An Abundant Life
More Precious Than Rubies

An Abundant Life
More Precious Than Rubies

Iris M. Williams

Copyright © 2020 by Iris M Williams. All rights reserved.

An attempt has been made to recreate events, locales and conversations from the author's memory of them. In order to maintain their anonymity, in some instances, the names of some individuals have been changed as well as some identifying characteristics and details such as physical properties, occupations, and places of residence.

This book or any portion thereof may not be reproduced or used in any manner whatsoever without the express written permission of Iris M Williams except for the use of brief quotations in a book review.

Printed in the United States of America.

First Printing, 2019

ISBN: 9781951883003

LCCN: 2019954796

Edited by Madison Lawson

Book Cover by Reta Laraway

Book Design by Ricky Allen/Relate LLC

The Butterfly Typeface Publishing

Little Rock Arkansas 72215

To every person who ever felt unloved, unworthy, and unrecognized.
God loves you. God values you. God sees you.

"You can't make sense of nonsense."

Iris M Williams

Content

Book I
Faith In Self

Prologue
    'Things Mama Said'..25

Chapter One
    'You Gotta Be a Big Girl'...29

Chapter Two
    'A New Blue Dress'..37

Chapter Three
    'Ignorant Ass Fool'..43

Chapter Four
    'Fix Yo Durn Face'...49

Chapter Five
    'Blessings'...53

Chapter Six
    'Unnoticed'..61

Chapter Seven
    'First Times'...65

Chapter Eight
    'Where Is My Mama?'..71

Chapter Nine
    'I'm Having a Baby'..77

Chapter Ten
    'A Ticking Time Bomb'..81

Chapter Eleven
    'A Reprieve'...85

Chapter Twelve
    'An Answered Prayer'...89

Epilogue
    'The Choices We Make'..95

Book II
Faith In No One

Prologue 107

Introduction
    'DeJa Vu' 109

Chapter One
    'Baby Jamie' 113

Chapter Two
    'Bradford James' 119

Chapter Three
    'Kerry Wilson' 125

Chapter Four
    'Anton Davis' 133

Chapter Five
    'William White' 143

Chapter Six
    'Gregg Harrison' 151

Chapter Seven
    'Donald Ingram' 159

Chapter Eight
    'Malcolm Devoe' 169

Chapter Nine
    'The Prophetess'..177
Chapter Ten
    'Starting Over, Again'...181
Epilogue
    'Going Home'..187

Book III
Faith In God

Prologue 201

Introduction
    'Faith in God' 203

Chapter One: SAD
    'Love Never Forgets' 209

Chapter Two: Purpose
    'Writing Saved My Life' 213

Chapter Three: Life
    'A Tribute' 217

Chapter Four: Standards
    'A Woman's Worth' 221

Chapter Five: Me Too
    'What Now?' 225

Chapter Six: Connected
    'Love Never Leaves' 229

Chapter Seven: Reflections
    'The Writing on The Wall' 233

Chapter Eight: Confessions
    'Testify' 241

Chapter Nine: Forgiveness

    'I Love You, Mama'..247

Chapter Ten: Giving Love

    'Innocence'...253

Epilogue: The Truth

    'More Precious Than Rubies'..261

Bonus Chapter: Finding Love

    'Wonder Twin Power'..269

About the Author..277

Book I
Faith In Self

For Mr. Jack
I Still Miss You

Foreword

For as long as I can remember, I never wanted to be looked at or recognized. I was comfortable blending into the background. In my mind, it was safer than to be upfront, the center of attention and under scrutiny.

I never took the time to analyze my life. I was too busy reading and escaping into the lives of others. After all, fantasy was much more pleasant than my own life.

When things happened, I somehow instinctively knew or perhaps was taught, to simply push it aside until there was a better, more appropriate time to think about it.

In the meantime, life kept happening, and with each new circumstance, situation, and challenge, I built a new wall of forbearance.

This was my way of coping. This was my way of being resilient. If I just pushed things to the side, I could move forward.

Well, it sounded good on paper anyway.

Eventually, life caught up.

There is only so much disappointment, heartbreak, and denial one person can endure before he or she is forced to face it, process it, and own it.

I tried hard to suppress my feelings of inadequacy, rejection, and self-loathing. Smiling when you don't feel happy takes more energy than it does to cry.

I was not encouraged or taught to express what I was feeling.

After more than 30 years of suppressing what was hurting me, I was still trying to be my daddy's 'big girl,' but finally, I just couldn't do it anymore.

And I began to cry.

The crying scared me because I wasn't used to it, but also because I was crying about things that I shouldn't have.

I was angry.

And I cried.

That's when I knew this was serious.

My therapist said, "Your box is full."

"What box?" I asked, wondering which one of us was the crazy one.

"You've been stuffing your feelings in a box for years. And now, there is no more room."

As it turns out, secrets grow larger in the dark.

I was taught that crying was a sign of weakness and that 'big girls' DO NOT cry.

So, what do 'big girls' do when they're hurt or sad?

I pushed my pain down and tried to forget about it.

The thing is, secrets don't die. They fester, but instead of rotting and decaying into nothingness, they rot (and stink) and grow so that they actually weigh more than they did going in.

One day I was at work and my festered hurts flew out of my eyes, onto my face, down my cheeks, across my belly, onto my lap, and slid into my shoes, causing me to stumble and fall. And when I tried to get up, I realized I was carrying the weight of my world in my shoes.

I slumped and slouched and moaned and groaned and even tried to run, but wherever I went, the weight was with me.

Until finally, I surrendered and let go of the secrets.

It was ugly. It stank. It hurt. It was sad.

But then I was free.

Finally, I could begin to live the life God intended for me – an abundant life.

I wrote this book for me, but I also wrote it for you. I want you to know that you can be free too.

My journey towards self-discovery began when I moved to North Carolina. It was the first time in my life that I was truly alone – no Mama, no children, no husband, no responsibility. I was unemployed.

It's not the drop from the top that hurts. It's the landing on rock bottom that does.

When you lose everything, you learn to appreciate everything.

In retrospect, I appreciate the things I lost – material things, friends, love … because now I know what's real.

Thank you to the people who see me and who give to me without regard for receiving. They know who they are because I tell them frequently.

To God be the glory!

#ButterflyBaby

Prologue

'Things Mama Said'

The things Mama said were not easy for me to understand.

Mama didn't always use the right words.

For instance, if it was cold outside and I didn't bundle up properly, Mama would say, "Put on yo hats and gloves 'fore you catch the new morning!"

Honestly, I didn't have a clue what the "new morning" was. Taking time to understand wasn't my first priority. Catching the new morning (whatever that was), wasn't my fear. I was most afraid of what would happen if I didn't comply with her instructions.

Immediately, I'd put on my hat and gloves.

I was probably in my first year of college before I realized that the new morning was actually pneumonia. And it's true that if you don't wear proper clothing in the winter, you can contract a bad cold or even pneumonia.

Many years later, I learned that while most of what Mama said was true, there were things that were not true.

Mama frequently called me an ignorant ass fool. Because she

didn't use the right words and she mumbled to me while she had mouthwash in her mouth, I was usually scrambling for clarity. From her perspective, I was an ignorant ass fool.

"Mmm. Mmmm. Mmmm," Mama mumbled as she swished Dr. Tichenor's Mouthwash around in her mouth. "Mmm. Mmm. Mmmm!"

Once again, I held back tears as I frantically searched my brain for what she could be saying. I never got it right, though. And as I stood there dumbfounded, she'd rush out of the room, spit out the mouthwash, and return to the room highly upset.

Smack!

"Go in the bedroom and get my shoes so I can go," Mama yelled. She was always so frustrated that I never seemed to know what she was saying – with or without the Dr. Tichenor's Mouthwash.

Honestly, I didn't understand it, either. As the youngest of thirteen, I felt like I was the only one who didn't understand Mama.

Mama spoke to everyone the same. So, why wasn't I getting it?

I was convinced that what Mam said about me was true. I was dumb. I was an ignorant ass fool.

Dear Diary,

I just want to be loved.

Iris

Then one year during my senior high school awards assembly, it dawned on me that perhaps I wasn't ignorant after all. I had consistently maintained the honor roll and was receiving numerous awards.

Was Mama wrong? No, I decided. These people just felt sorry for me. Or, maybe they were mistaken. I smiled and accepted the awards, but in the back of mind, I knew it wouldn't be long before they realized their mistake and came to take the awards back.

It took years for me to accept the fact that I wasn't dumb. But that revelation came too late. The damage had already been done.

Even when faced with overwhelming proof, it's hard to undo years of hurt, disappointment, and abuse.

I had a singular view of my world. Mama was right and everyone else was wrong.

To this day, it's hard to forget the things Mama said.

I find it difficult to accept compliments and I'm always afraid that people will figure out the truth about me.

I am an ignorant ass fool.

Chapter One

'You Gotta Be a Big Girl'

I'd always been Mr. Jack's big girl and I wanted to be.

"I've got something to tell ya, but you gotta promise me you won't cry," Mama said to me. "You gotta be a big girl for Mr. Jack."

I diverted my eyes to the white wall behind Mama. It was a stark contrast to the life I lived. Clean, bright, and uncluttered.

I nodded my six-year-old head up and down. It was still early, so I guess that's why Mama didn't hit me for nodding instead of saying yes out loud.

Our trailer was already starting to heat up. It was August, and the Arkansas sun was already shining brightly. I was wondering why I didn't smell bacon, and why we weren't about to have breakfast. Something was wrong.

"Mr. Jack is dead," Mama said as if she'd told me that my older brother ate the last of the breakfast while I was sleeping.

Based on Mama's disposition, I knew instinctively that being 'dead' wasn't a good thing for Mr. Jack to be. And although I didn't understand, I wanted to cry. I was a sensitive child and Mama hated that about me. She was always telling me to stop crying. The look on her face confirmed that crying wouldn't be tolerated. Besides, I'd already promised I wouldn't. Mama was looking at me. I looked back at the white wall.

After a few seconds, Mama got up and began busying herself with her daily tasks. I followed her around for a time, hoping there would be more information about Mr. Jack and him being dead. But there wasn't, and soon Mama got irritated.

"Gal, go somewhere and play," Mama said. "I got work to do."

Mama was always working. The only time she sat or smiled was on the phone with her many friends or when Mr. Jack was around. Mama's smile faded around the same time Mr. Jack decided to go be dead.

Mama sent me outside, but the farthest I ever went was the front steps. I hated being outside. It was hot, smelly, and scary. Stray dogs, bugs, and the heat kept me wishing I could be inside.

As I sat on the steps and thought about Mr. Jack and him being dead, I decided Mama must have been wrong. I didn't feel like Mr. Jack was dead. Would I know something like that?

So, I waited. Maybe he had just left really early before breakfast. But he didn't come back for lunch or dinner. And when Mama insisted I go to bed that night, I began to worry.

Where was he?

The next morning at breakfast, Mr. Jack's chair was empty again.

I missed his huge, big toothy smile and slow conversation.

This morning, we ate in silence.

Lunchtime came and I quietly waited again by the front door for Mr. Jack to come home. I was hoping that for once, Mama was wrong.

But Mr. Jack never showed up for lunch, and that night at dinner his chair was still empty.

After dinner, I did my best to stay awake. I looked at our black and white television, but I wasn't paying attention to the program. I was listening for Mr. Jack's truck. I was hoping he'd come home any minute and tell me it was time for bed. I wanted him to tuck me in like he always did.

"It's past time for you to be in the bed, gal," Mama said, jarring me out of my memory. She'd been on the phone with one of her many friends. "Go on now and get in the bed. Goodnight."

I knew better than to argue or cry, so I stood up slowly and walked down the long, dark hallway to my bedroom. I pulled back the covers, climbed into bed, and slowly pulled the covers up over my head.

It was clear that Mr. Jack wasn't coming back.

I realized that being dead meant you don't come home. I decided that being dead was definitely not a good thing.

The next morning at breakfast, I stared at Mr. Jack's empty chair and thought about the last time we'd all had breakfast.

"Maybeline, you know you can cook!" He said and flashed that big, toothy smile at me. "Can't she Chico-stick?"

I nodded my head and smiled right back. Chico-stick was Mr. Jack's nickname for me. Every day when he came home for lunch, he'd bring me a brown paper bag full of candies. My favorite was the chic-o-sticks.

"One day, you're gonna cook your daddy some good food too , ain't ya Chico-Stick?"

I nodded again.

"Open up yo mouf and talk," Mama yelled. "You act like you deef and dumb!" Mama hated for me to nod.

"No," I said as the smile on my face disappeared. "I mean, yes." Now I was nervous and whenever I was nervous, I'd always say the wrong thing.

Mama looked at me and shook her head. "Hurry up and eat yo food so ya can go outside."

Mama didn't like talking at the table or kids being inside. I hated being outside, except when I was with Mr. Jack. He'd let me ride on his shoulders. I was away from the bugs, the stray dogs, and the rocks that hurt my bare feet. On his shoulders, I felt like a princess.

"Aw she aight Maybeline," Mr. Jack said to Mama.

"No, the gal need to know how to open her mouth and talk and quit acting like she don't know how to talk." Mama shot me an angry glance and headed into the kitchen.

"When she ready to talk, she will." Mr. Jack called out to her. Then he patted a spot on his lap. I scooted back from the table so fast my chair fell backward.

"What is all that racket in there!" Mama yelled from the kitchen.

"Just me Maybeline," Mr. Jack called to Mama. "I got it."

I looked toward the kitchen afraid Mama would see that it was really me who knocked the chair over. Mr. Jack helped me with the chair. Then I sat on his lap. He gave me a hug and a kiss on the cheek.

Mr. Jack was always rescuing me. Who would save me from Mama now?

"Eat yo food before it gets cold, gal. We got to go to town." Mama's voice interrupted my thoughts. "We ain't got time for you to be daydreaming."

I loved bacon, and normally, breakfast was my favorite. But this morning, the eggs, bacon, and potatoes may as well be cardboard. I ate it anyway because I knew Mama would be mad if I didn't. "Waste not, want not," she always said.

After breakfast, me and Mama caught a ride into town. Mama didn't drive so we were always catching rides from one of her friends.

We got dropped off in town and walked to the bank and to Fred's grocery store to pay something on her bill.

Mama surprised me too and bought me a pretty blue dress from Buck Won's. Everything in the store smelled like Chinese, but their prices were the best in town.

"What you need ma'am," Mr. Buck Won asked Mama. Mama said he and his family had lived in Holly Grove since she was a little girl, but he still didn't speak English good. "I get for you."

"I jes need this here dress for my gal," Mama said and put the dress on the counter. It was the color of the sky and had a belt that tied around the waist. "I think it will fit her bony butt."

Mama was always talking about how skinny I was and that she was going to have to get me some vitamins so I'd eat.

I looked down at my legs and realized there were skinny.

When we finished our errands, we walked to Mama's best friend, Ms. Helene.

Ms. Helene had a lot of kids like Mama, and the two of them had been friends forever.

"Leen, I'm sorry to hear about Jack." Ms. Helene said calling Mama by her nickname. She leaned over from her chair and spit in a small metal can. "He was a good mane."

I loved to visit Ms. Helene's house. It was alive. There was noise, people coming in and out, and kids for me to play with.

"Thank ya Helene," Mama said, looking sad. "I don't know what I'm gonna do without Jack. He was my backbone."

Ms. Helene spat in her can again. The brown spit smelled strong. Sometimes she would spit far off the porch and into the yard.

I tried spitting that way at home once, but it just landed on the front of my shirt. Mama smacked me real good for doing that. Later when she told Mr. Jack, he laughed so hard that Mama ended up laughing too.

Mr. Jack was the only person that made Mama laugh like that. She laughed sometimes with her friends, but not like she did with Mr. Jack.

"When the fune gone be?" Ms. Helene asked my Mama.

"I think I heard it gonna be Sa'day," Mama said, and she looked even sadder. "I don't think we gon go, tho. I don't want no mess."

"Chile, I wouldn't care about no mess," Ms. Helene said. "You loved that mane, and he loved you. Wouldn't nun keep me way from there!"

"I guess I will," Mama agreed. "Jack be mad ef I didn't go."

I heard what they were saying, but I didn't understand most of it. I didn't know what a 'fune' was, but whatever it was, it made Mama sad. And it made Ms. Helene mad.

I went to sit under the tree while Mama and Ms. Helene talked. I knew her kids would be home from school soon.

I had missed my first year of school because I had hip surgery. I was up and walking now though, and I was ready to go to school. Mama had arranged for me to get my lessons at home so I would still pass kindergarten, but I wanted to go to school to be with the other kids.

Ms. Helene's kids were my only friends. They taught me a lot of stuff including how to Chinese jump rope. Mama didn't like me jumping rope. She said it wasn't good for my hip. I didn't want the other kids to know I couldn't jump rope, so I always convinced them to jump in Ms. Helene's backyard instead.

I sat on the stump and looked back at Mama and Ms. Helene. Mama had just got her hair done; it was real shiny and black. Her curls hung soft to her shoulders. Ms. Helene wore her hair very short and in an afro. She always looked so comfortable and happy. Today, she wore a pair of lime green capris and a crisp white sleeveless top. Mama never wore capris because she said she had broken veins. I looked down at my legs to check for broken veins. I didn't see any.

I heard the kids before I saw them and stood up. Ms. Helene's kids came running around the fence. School was finally out. I hoped we could jump rope before Mama's and my ride came to take us home.

"Get in the house and take them school clothes off and go get started on dinner," Ms. Helene called out to her kids.

"But we was gonna jump rope and play with Iris," Janine said.

An Abundant Life, Faith in Self

"No, you ain't. It ain't Saday," Ms. Helene reminded her. "Y'all gotta get dinner, do your lesson, get baths, and get ready for school tomorrow."

I sat back down. I was sad to hear we couldn't jump rope. I looked at Mama and she was looking at me. But I didn't say nothing.

Janine and her older sister, Carol Anne, went inside like their Mama told them, but Louvelle, their younger brother, ran past his Mama. Ms. Helene jumped up to run after him, but he was too fast. Soon, he was out of the yard and out of sight.

"Louvelle!" Ms. Helene called out. "You betta get yo ass back here and help these girls!"

Louvelle kept going. We could hear him laughing and we knew where he was going. A lot of the kids went to the town park after school to play.

I thought Ms. Helene was gonna be mad, but she wasn't. She spat and sat back down next to Mama.

"Leen, I don't know what I'mma do with that red tail boy." She laughed. "Ef I say go left, he takes his ass right."

They both laughed and kept right on talking. I saw Janine and Carol Anne peek out the curtain at me and motion for me to come inside. I got up and quickly walked past Mama and Ms. Helene.

Janine and Carol Anne were mixing and chopping food like Mama did when she was in the kitchen. I didn't know how to cook. Mama never allowed me in her kitchen.

Dear Diary

I wish I understand where Mr. Jack was.

He's been gone for a week now and I miss him so much.

I've been a big girl like Mama told me. I haven't cried.

Today Mama said we were going to see Mr. Jack!

I can't wait.

Iris

"You sad?" Janine asked me.

"No," I said. "Why you ask me that?"

"Cuz yo daddy died guhl," Carol Anne said and both girls looked at me strangely.

"Ef it was my daddy, I'd still be crying," Janine said. "I wouldn't stop."

Now I wanted to cry. I missed Mr. Jack and wanted him to not be dead. But I promised Mama that I'd be a big girl.

"Iris," Mama yelled into the house. "Com on, our ride here!"

I was glad it was time to leave because I didn't want to talk to them about Mr. Jack. I didn't want to explain why I couldn't cry.

That night as I walked the long dark hallway alone, pulled back my covers, and climbed into bed, I wanted to cry very badly.

I didn't know if Mr. Jack was gonna stay dead or if it was just for a little while. I felt so lost and confused.

I pulled the covers up to my chin.

Mama said big girls don't cry. She said I had to be a big girl for Mr. Jack.

So, I wouldn't cry.

Chapter Two

'A New Blue Dress'

I woke up excited. Mama said we were going to church and I could wear the new blue dress she bought me from town. She said I was going to see Mr. Jack, too.

She hot combed my hair and pulled it up into a tight ponytail on top of my head. As I slipped into my new dress, the new smell really made me happy.

"Come on, gal," Mama yelled. "Our ride is here."

Mr. Buddy John and his wife Mrs. Hatt sat in the car, already sweating from the August sun. In the car ride, I sat in the back seat and looked out the window. The sky was as blue as the dress I was wearing. Blue was Mr. Jack's favorite color, and now it was my favorite, too.

"I don't think I'm gonna go in," Mama told Mr. Buddy John. "I don't like funes."

"I don't blame you, Leen," Mr. Buddy John said. "It might be for the best, anyway."

"Take her in there and let her view the body," Mama told Mr. Buddy John.

"You sure you want to do that, Leen?" Mr. Buddy John asked. "That's a lot for a child …"

"She needs to go in and see him," Mama said. "She gon be alright."

I didn't know what they were saying. I knew it was about me. I wanted to ask questions, but Mama didn't like questions, so I sat quietly.

We pulled into the church lot and Mr. Buddy John parked behind the church. There were a lot of cars. Everyone was wearing black. I wondered why I wasn't wearing black, too. But I liked my blue dress better.

I got out of the car and walked beside Mr. Buddy John. Mrs. Hattie Mae stayed in the car with Mama.

As soon as we walked into the church, I could feel all eyes on me. I think they were all waiting to see if I was going to cry. Mama had reminded me again the night before that I had to continue to be a big girl. So, I was not going to cry.

I had on my new blue dress. It made me feel happy and pretty. Mama said I could wear it on the first day of school in a few weeks, too.

Me and Mr. Buddy John sat down, and I looked around at the people who were there. Everyone looked so sad.

That's when I saw it.

At the front of the church was a big, shiny, blue box. I looked closer and realized Mr. Jack was lying in the box.

Was he sleeping?

I smiled. I was about to see Mr. Jack again. I started to get up, but Mr. Buddy John shook his head, so I sat back down.

People were doing a lot of talking and singing and then the preacher told us all to stand up. We got in a line and began walking to the front of the church where Mr. Jack was sleeping.

As we walked up to the big, shiny, blue box, I saw Mr. Jack laying there in a new black suit. His hair was combed real nice, and he had on his mason pin. I knew what it was because he'd shown it to me before. He told me he only wore it on special occasions. I guess this was special.

Mr. Jack had on his glasses but his eyes were closed. I remember he used to go to sleep lots of times with his glasses on. Mama always took them off so he wouldn't break them. Mama wasn't here, so who would take them off?

Mr. Jack's face was clean and smooth. He would always shave on Sundays before church.

Sunday morning was my favorite day of the week. While Mr. Jack would shave, I'd sit on the closed toilet seat and watch him slide the razor across his face. He never cut himself, either.

"What you gonna be when you grow up, Chico-stick?"

"I'mma be a farmer like you, Mr. Jack."

"Naw, that's what I am," he explained. "I want to know what you wanna be."

The nurses at the hospital were all so nice and their white dresses, shoes, and hat were always crisp and clean. They always took real good care of me.

"I want to be a nurse," I said. "I want to help people feel better."

Mr. Buddy John pushed me and I remembered we were in church, so I tried to pay attention. We were close now and the people in line ahead of us were stopping to stare at Mr. Jack. Some wiped their eyes.

Finally, it was my turn. I stood there and waited for Mr. Jack to open his eyes. He didn't. He didn't move either.

Is this what dead means? I didn't like it. I wanted to cry. Maybe I could since Mama wasn't here. Then I looked up and saw Ms. Helene. She saw me too and I knew she would tell Mama.

Mr. Buddy John pushed me forward in the line.

Instead of going back to our seat, we went to the car where Mama and Mrs. Hattie Mae were inside talking.

"How was it," Mama asked Mr. Buddy John.

"He looked real good," Mr. Buddy John said. "He looked just like hisself."

No, he didn't. He was dark and stiff. He wasn't smiling, either. I never saw Mr. Jack looking like that.

Why did Mr. Buddy John say that?

Mama said children weren't supposed to call grown folks a lie, but he had.

"It was a real nice fune," Mr. Buddy John said.

Although no one told me, I figured out that Mr. Jack was going to stay dead.

"I still think you should've went in," Mrs. Hattie Mae said to Mama. "You needed to say goodbye."

Goodbye? I didn't know I was supposed to say goodbye. I wanted to go back inside and say goodbye. As Mr. Buddy John drove off the church parking lot, I got on my knees and looked out the back window.

I saw the big, shiny, blue box Mr. Jack was in being taken from the church and put inside a long black car. I knew I would never see Mr. Jack again. I wanted to cry.

"Turn around, gal," Mama yelled. "Get yo knees out the seat."

I did what she told me.

"I said bye to Jack when he died," Mama said. "I didn't need to go in to say it. I don't want to remember him that way, anyway."

I looked at Mama. She was looking out her side of the window. She pulled a handkerchief from her purse and wiped her eyes.

The drive home was long. Mr. Buddy John and his wife talked, but me and Mama didn't say anything.

Dear Diary,

There is a lot I cannot remember, and I wish I could remember.

Mama says I'm dumb.

It must be true since there is so much I don't know.

Iris

I had never seen Mama so quiet. I think she was crying, but why was it ok for her to cry and not me? Where was Mr. Jack going? Why was he in that box and why didn't someone tell me to say goodbye?

This was such an odd day.

I scooted next to Mama and lay my head on her shoulders.

"Move," Mama said. "It's too hot for you to be sitting so close to me."

I should've known better. Even though the windows were all down, it was still hot inside the car. Mama told me there were times she didn't want her own hands to touch her. So, I understood why she wouldn't want me to.

I missed Mr. Jack. I felt like crying, but I didn't dare. Suddenly, I felt alone.

Who would talk to me and laugh with me?

Mama never did, except to yell at me. She talked to her friends, but not to me. I was just a 'shittin ass kid'.

"Leen, don't you fret none," Mrs. Hattie Mae said to Mama. "Jack up in Heaven now with the Good Lord."

I looked out the window at the sky. It was so blue. The clouds were big, and they were so white and puffy. They looked so close that I thought if I reached out the window, I could touch one.

I closed my eyes and thought about Mr. Jack. This was the kind of day he would have loved.

"Look at the sky, Chico-stick," he would say. "The Good Lord really knows how to care for His people."

I didn't feel so bad knowing that Mr. Jack was in Heaven with the Good Lord. I knew the Good Lord was taking real good care of Mr. Jack.

Iris M. Williams

Mama made sure that Mr. Buddy John and Mrs. Hattie Mae came in to have supper with us when we got home. I sat at the table with them. They laughed and talked, but I stared at the front door.

Mr. Jack would never walk through that door again.

Then I looked over at the wall next to the door.

It was clean, crisp, and bare.

There were no pictures, no color, no life.

Chapter Three

'Ignorant Ass Fool'

Going to the doctor was something I never looked forward to.

"Her hymen has been broken," Dr. Buckhead told my mother.

I didn't know what that meant but judging from the look on my mother's face, I knew that it wasn't good.

Mama looked at me and I looked away. I didn't know what was happening. Since the day before, I'd been a nervous wreck.

"We're going to see Dr. Buckhead," Mama said with one hand on her hip and in the other she held out a pair of my panties. "You ain't got no business with all this discharge in yo pannies."

Our town, Holly Grove, was small and rural and nothing went on that people in the town didn't know.

Mama had been born here and so had her mama. The town had a post office, gas station, more than a dozen churches, two grocery stores, a bank, and one physician, Dr. Stone.

Ever since Mr. Jack died, we didn't go to Dr. Stone. For some reason, Mama decided that Dr. Stone wasn't a good doctor anymore. And although Dr. Stone had delivered all of her children, suddenly he wasn't to be trusted. Now, we had to go see Dr. Buckhead in Clarendon who was nearly twenty miles away.

Dr. Buckhead, like Dr. Stone, was an older white man. I liked Dr. Stone. I knew him and he was nice. He spoke softly and always gave me a sucker when Mama and I left his office. Dr. Buckhead was a big man, he had white hair, wore thick glasses and his big white hands were always cold. They felt like ice on my skin.

He was touching me now and I wanted to scream.

Dr. Buckhead looked at Mama. Mama looked at me, and I looked away. The wall behind Dr. Buckhead was white. Dr. Stone's office was warm and friendly. There were pictures of children playing. This room was empty, cold, and lacked feeling.

I wished I were anywhere but here.

Somehow, my brain had long since outgrown my ten-year-old body. And although I was wise beyond my years to things I couldn't even begin to comprehend, there were still things that made no sense.

"Whut that mean?" Mama asked Dr. Buckhead.

I was sure it was for the benefit of my further embarrassment. Judging by the hate in her eyes, I knew she already knew what a broken hymen was.

"It means she's had sex." He replied. His glare was hard and cold. I could feel him wanting to add, "What a shame and disappointment she turned out to be."

Thanks to Mr. Jack being dead when I was six, I knew what death and funerals were. And thanks to Mrs. Holcombe, my fifth-grade teacher, I learned about periods and boys. So, I knew what sex was, but I didn't recall having it as Dr. Buckhead said I had.

Why would he say that?

Mama said kids weren't supposed to call grown folks a lie. But he lied.

Didn't he?

I was so confused. I wracked my brain trying to remember having sex, but I couldn't.

We were barely into summer vacation and unlike most kids, I was already ready for school to begin again. I loved school because I loved reading and learning. It was the only place in our town where I could get my hands on a good book. The library was closed during summer vacation.

We had a new librarian. Miss Peaches was a huge lady. She had a large round body, tiny arms and legs, and a very small head. She wore her hair in a tight, neat bun and wore bright red lipstick. The other kids laughed and made fun of her behind her back, but I liked her. She had kind eyes and always spoke in a soft voice.

"You there girl, come here," Miss Peaches called out to me.

"Yes, ma'am?" I hurried over to her.

"What's wrong with your leg?" She asked with what felt like concern. "Do you need to go to the nurse?"

"Oh, nothing, ma'am," I responded and turned to leave. Miss Peaches was new to our town. She didn't know that I'd been crippled (as Mama called it) my whole life.

"Wait a minute. So, if it's nothing, why are you limping?" She asked.

I was about to tell her what Mama had told me – that I was born with a 'bad hip' and that even after 13 surgeries, it was still raggedy. But Terry Richardson beat me to the explanation.

"She was born that way, Miss Peaches!" Terry yelled out before I could answer. The other kids snickered. I was embarrassed and wanted to cry, but instead, I held my head down and hurried from the library.

It was hard being different. I wished I had another person to talk to, but I didn't. I wished there was someone who understood, but there wasn't. I wished I could be anywhere but here, but I wasn't. That's why I loved books so much. Reading offered an escape from a world where I didn't belong.

In books, people were whole, happy, and loved. In books, the lives of others were a thousand times better than mine.

How I missed Mr. Jack. If he were here, things would be so different. He would hold my hand and ask me if I was ok. With Mr. Jack, I could even cry. Then he'd hold me tight and tell me that everything was 'awright'. And with him, things were alright too. But since his death, nothing had been the same and I feared nothing ever would.

"I knew she had too much dischurge in her pannys." Mama's hateful words jolted me back to my present embarrassment.

Dr. Buckhead and Mama continued to talk while I lay there on that crinkly, hard, white paper that betrayed me every time I tried to move. I could feel the gel he used ooze from inside me onto the paper underneath. I wanted to ask if it was ok to get up, clean myself, and put my clothes back on, but I knew better than to interrupt Mama. So, I just laid there and stared at the white wall.

The white wall stared back. I had come to envy the white wall. There, nothing ever happened, and things remained the same.

I desperately wanted my life to be dull and boring where things never happened or showed.

I missed Mr. Jack.

Since he left, I hadn't been hugged or kissed. Mama didn't say "I love you" and she didn't laugh with me. She didn't tuck me into bed, bring me candy, or ask me what I wanted to be.

I was Mr. Jack's 'big girl,' but I desperately wanted to be my mama's baby. I wanted to cry, be sad, and be a kid.

"Get up gal and put on yo clothes so we can get outta here,"

Mama said with disdain.

"Yes ma'am," I mumbled.

Dr. Buckhead left the room, and soon his nurse returned with several small slips of paper. She explained to Mama that I had an infection and would have to take medication for 7 to 10 days and that I was to come back in 2 weeks for a follow-up visit.

The ride home was going to be a long one.

I decided again that Mama was right. I was dumb. Who has sex and doesn't remember?

An Abundant Life, Faith in Self

"Buddy John, can you run me by the drug sto so I can get this guhl her medicine?" Mama asked Mr. Buddy John. "It won't take long, and I will buy you and Mrs. Hattie Mae a cool drank. What kind ya want?"

Mr. Buddy John nodded his head. He was a huge man with huge features. He had piercing eyes that I was convinced could see clean through a soul – well mine anyway.

His wife, Mrs. Hattie Mae, was sickly and had to go to Little Rock three times a week for dialysis treatments. Her arms were always covered with band-aids. Her long, straight black hair was sticking to her forehead, and she was already drinking a cold bottle of Pepsi. She smiled at me, and I smiled back. Mrs. Hattie Mae was one of the few adults who ever smiled at me.

I climbed into the back seat with Mama. The seat burned the back of my legs. I wished I had a towel to sit on.

With all the windows down, it was hard for Mama to have a conversation. As Mr. Buddy John started the car and began driving to the drug store, Mama leaned forward so Mrs. Hattie Mae could hear her over the wind blowing into the car.

"Dr. Buckhead said she been having sex." Mama shouted to Mrs. Hattie Mae. "I knew something wun't right."

I lay my head back onto the seat and pretended to go to sleep. I knew Mama didn't love me, and I couldn't blame her. I was an 'ignorant ass fool'. I had to be. Who has sex at 10-years-old and worse yet, doesn't even remember it?

Dear Diary,

Mama hates me because I'm not strong like her.

Screaming, crying, and being sad is what I feel like, but I can't let it out.

I miss Mr. Jack.

I need someone to give me a hug and tell me they love me.

Iris

Chapter Four

'Fix Yo Durn Face'

WAM!

Out of nowhere, the whole left side of my face began stinging. Instinctively, I put my hands up to my face and peeked out at her between my fingers. Now, what have I done wrong? I wondered.

"Fix yo durn face!" Mama said harshly between tight lips.

Before I could say anything, she pushed me back a few steps so that no one could see us.

"I know you know better than to act like you don't have any sense up here in this church!"

"Yes, ma'am," I answered, but I still didn't know what I'd done wrong.

Mama had her own way of teaching me right from wrong. Her number one teaching tool was her hand. Today's lesson was that it's better to not have feelings than to let them show on your face.

Mama's half-sister, Aunt Ethelene Mae who dipped snuff and always had snuff and spit in the corner of her mouth, was about to put her snuff-smeared lips on my cheeks. Pastor White didn't allow spit jars in the church, so Aunt Ethelene's cheeks would fill up with spit, and some would dribble from her lips.

Aunt Ethelene Mae was a kisser. But I didn't want her kissing me. When I saw her coming, I turned to run and had run right into Mama.

"Now you turn around and give Aunt Ethelene a hug," Mama commanded.

I turned around slowly and went back to Aunt Ethelene. I stood still and 'fixed my face' while she leaned down to kiss me. She smelled of Vicks Vapor-rub, snuff, and hair grease.

After Aunt Ethelene was done, I walked slowly to the church bathroom to wash my face.

Iris M. Williams

I could feel Aunt Ethelene's spit on my cheek.

Church wasn't the only place where I had to make sure I looked a certain way. Anytime we were around other people, Mama made sure that I smiled whether I felt like it or not.

After church, we caught a ride home so Mama could finish her Sunday dinner. We always had company for Sunday dinner.

I heard a car pull into our yard and went to see who it was.

"Mama," I yelled. "Uncle Mister and Aunt Sister pulling up."

"Well, go open the door and let them in," Mama hollered.

Uncle Mister and Aunt Sister went to our church, too. They were older and didn't have any children, so Mama always invited them over for supper after church.

"Come on in," Mama said wiping her hands on her apron.

Uncle Mister was a bent man. His back was bent. His legs were bowed, and his fingers were bent at the tips, too. He wore the same clothes every day, even on Sunday. Uncle Mister had two teeth, and they were at the bottom.

His wife, Aunt Effie, was a dark-skinned woman. She always wore hats, gloves, and brown stockings. She laughed a lot, even when nothing was funny, so Mama called her crazy.

"We sho thank you for having us over for supper again," Aunt Effie laughed. "One day you gon' have to come to our house for supper."

I had heard Mama talking about Uncle Mister and Aunt Sister's home on many occasions.

"It's a durn shame Mister and Sister living like hogs," Mama told Ms. Helene once.

"Leen, you crazy," Ms. Helene'd snickered. "Why you say that?"

"They is," Mama laughed too. "The flo is dirty as the ground, it stank in there, and they keep the doors and windows shut so tight it's hard to breathe."

What Mama said and what Mama did didn't always match. She told Ms. Helene that she would never step foot in Uncle Mister and Aunt Sister's home. Now, she was

An Abundant Life, Faith in Self

saying something different.

"Thank you, Effie," Mama said. "I would love that, but y'all my elders and Pastor White say we are to take care of y'all."

"Well, maybe sometimes you can let yo girl come and spend the night with us," Aunt Effie said.

They all looked at me, and I frowned. Going to Uncle Mister and Aunt Sister's house to do anything was NOT something I wanted to do.

I continued to frown and shake my head back and forth.

"Y'all can go wash yo hands now," Mama told Uncle Mister and Aunt Sister. "Supper ready now."

As soon as they walked out of the room, Mama's hand came out of nowhere and smacked me hard.

"Fix yo durn face," Mama said.

"Yes ma'am," I said. I still hadn't learned which of my faces Mama didn't like.

Mama stared at me like she was waiting for me to say more. I thought I saw sadness but just as quickly as it appeared it disappeared, and she scowled at me instead.

I looked away to the white wall.

There was something familiar about it now, comforting even.

I could count on the white wall to have no opinion of me at all.

Dear Diary,

Auntie Elvira shouted again today.

Mama said that Reverend Dover and Auntie Elvira need to quit playing with the Lord.

I don't know why we go to church ALL the time, and when we come home Mama still mean. Is she playing?

I used to pray real hard, but it didn't work, so I don't anymore. I'm kind of scared of God.

Is God like Mama?

If I don't do what he says, will he ignore me too?

Iris

Mama had a whole lot of rules.

I wished she'd write them down and give them to me to study.

She would hit me and long after the sting went away, I was still trying to figure out what I'd done wrong.

By trial and error, I learned that Mama expected me to dress appropriately, speak correctly, and act like I had sense.

The lesson with my face was that I needed to hide my emotions from my face. Emotions were only safe inside my head.

I was not to speak them aloud or show them.

Chapter Five

'Blessings'

The people who wore white were back.

"Be quiet and get down!" Mama said in a hushed tone.
I followed her lead and got down on the floor. From where I sat, I could see them approaching our front door. My heart was beating fast. Even though this was something that happened frequently, I never got used to it.

KNOCK!

KNOCK!

KNOCK!

I looked at Mama, and she looked at me with such anger. I quickly looked away and at the white wall. After what seemed like hours, the group of people dressed in white finally gave up and walked away from our house.

"I wish them durn people would get the hint," Mama said struggling to get up, "and stop knocking on my durn door!"

I sat there on the floor, still too afraid to move. For as long as I could remember, we didn't open the door when the strangers came knocking. We always hid from them.

"Why are we hiding," I asked Mama once.

She called me ignorant and nearly knocked me across the room. I figured it was something I was supposed to know already. So, I never asked her about them again.

In church, Reverend Dover said, "God blesses those who love their neighbors! And we should not only love our neighbors, but we should treat them the way we would want to be treated."

Weren't the people in white our neighbors, too? Wouldn't it be a blessing to love them instead of hiding from them?

I didn't want to be treated like we were treating them. And I wanted to be blessed.

One day the people in white came while Mama was in town. Mama had left strict instructions on what I was supposed to do while she was gone.

"Don't you open my door while I'm gone," Mama said.

"Yes, ma'am," I responded.

"And don't you be outside either," Mama said.

"Yes, ma'am," I said.

"And don't you be doing nothing you not supposed to," Mama warned.

"I won't," I said.

Mama left to go on her errand, and I went to my room to read my book.

KNOCK!

KNOCK!

KNOCK!

I ran to the living room and pulled back the curtain wide.

I saw them.

They saw me.

I was terrified.

KNOCK!

KNOCK!

KNOCK!

It was too late for me to act like I didn't see them.

"Hello," one of them said. "Can you open the door and let us in?"

"I can't," I said. Then clapped my hand over my mouth.

"It's ok," another one of them responded. "We just want to leave some information with you to give to your mother about Jehovah."

"Who's Jehovah?" I asked.

"Jehovah is God's real name," the lady said.

I looked back out at them, and the lady smiled at me. She held up a small piece of paper. There was a picture of Jesus on it. It was the same picture from our church.

I opened the door and stood in the doorway.

"I can't let you in," I said. "My mama isn't here."

"It's ok," the lady said. "We just want to leave this track here with you."

She handed me a small, thick pamphlet. And again, she smiled at me. I smiled back. Her smiled reminded me of Mr. Jack and Mrs. Hattie Mae.

"God bless you, child," she said.

No adult had bothered to bless me before. I wanted to let her in, but I knew better.

"I gotta close the door now," I told her. "My mama will be real mad if she comes home and sees you here."

I closed the door and went to the window. I pulled back the curtain and watched them continue down the road. They were talking and singing and smiling.

Then I went back to my bedroom and looked at the track they'd given me. There was

Jesus and what looked like Heaven. Heaven looked like a happy place. I wondered if Mr. Jack was in this Heaven and if he was happy.

I read the information. It said that God loved us and that in Heaven we would all be happy and there would be no more pain. It sounded like a great place.

When I finished reading, I slid the track inside one of my books. Mama would be mad me if she knew I let them in, but she'd be really angry if she knew I'd read their track.

The next Sunday at church, Reverend Dover's sermon was about Hell. Reverend Dover preached about Hell a lot.

"If you don't get to know the Lord," he shouted, "you will surely burn in Hell!"

The church clapped and some of the women hollered.

"You better get right with the Lord," Reverend Dover continued. "Or you won't get your reward."

Again, the church clapped, women screamed, and the piano player hammered out a tune.

"Time is getting short, church." Reverend Dover wiped the sweat from his forehead. "God is coming back for a church without a spot or blemish."

The church went into an uproar. People were jumping, screaming, and crying. No one looked happy about the Lord coming back. They didn't seem happy to go to Heaven.

I was terrified and confused.

I needed to find out how to know the Lord. I needed to know if I was right. I needed to know which Heaven I would go to.

Did I have spots and blemishes? Is that why Mama was so adamant about me scratching?

"Quit scratchin," she'd yell. "You'll make marks!"

Mama had a thing about skin. She didn't think it should be dark, ashy, or marked up. I had plenty of scars from all the surgeries on my hips. Maybe that's why Mama didn't like me.

I had so many questions, but there was no one I could ask them to. Then I remembered the information the people wearing white gave me.

When I got home, I told Mama I wasn't hungry, and I went straight to my room.

I read the information again, trying hard to understand.

The God Reverend Dover spoke about was scary, but the God in these tracks seemed loving.

Which one was real?

I wanted to know more.

I began telling Mama that I didn't want to go to town with her on Saturdays. Instead, I'd wait for the people in white to come. I didn't let them in no more, but as soon as I saw them leave, I'd open the door and get the track they left on our steps.

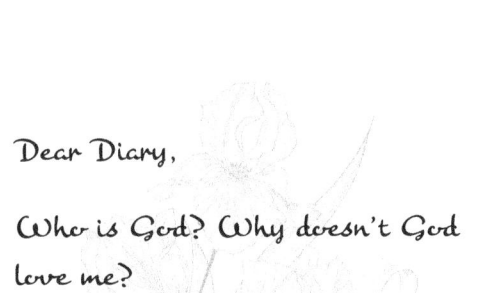

Dear Diary,

Who is God? Why doesn't God love me?

Iris

The more I read, the more I wanted to know.

Reverend Dover talked about blessings, but he didn't say how to get them. The blessings I read about in the track sounded so wonderful. I realized I wasn't blessed.

Blessings were good things and good things didn't happen to me. I was born crippled. Mr. Jack died, and Mama didn't love me.

I didn't think I knew anyone who was blessed.

On Sundays, the people at church cried and hollered and spoke about how much they loved God and how much He loved them. So why were they crying and looking so sad?

Outside of church they were mean, unhappy people who said and did awful things to each other.

But the people who we hid from were happy. They smiled and spoke about love.

I wasn't afraid of them the way Mama said I should be. But they did confuse me.

I hoped Mr. Jack was in the happy Heaven like the one the people who wore white spoke about.

To me, that would be a blessing.

I wanted to ask Mama about this, but I knew she would smack me if I told her what I'd been doing.

Then Mama announced she had a blessing of her own.

"We're moving," Mama said.

"Where are we going?" I asked.

"The Lord has blessed us with a place to live uptown," Mama said. "Now I can walk to where I need to go, and we won't have to catch rides."

I was happy we were moving uptown. I would be closer to my friend. But then I remembered that that was where my memories of Mr. Jack were, and I got sad. And I would have to stop talking to the people in white. Uptown people would know if I let them in and would tell Mama.

"God has answered my prayers," Mama continued. "What a blessing this is."

We moved uptown. There was no indoor plumbing and worst of all, I no longer had my own room. Me and Mama shared a room and a bed.

There were neighbors all around us and I felt like I was being watched every second.

There was a park behind our house, but Mama never let me go. She said the children were wild and I didn't need to be hanging around them.

So, I sat on our back porch and listened to the other kids run and play and laugh.

Maybe I had the wrong idea about blessings.

Chapter Six

'Unnoticed'

Whenever Mason came to visit, things got tense.

"Come here."

My cousin was tall and cute. His blue eyes and light skin made all the girls at school ooohh and ahhhh over him.

I did what he asked.

"Put your hands down here," he said.

I did what he asked.

He pulled the elastic waist band away from his body. I didn't want to make him mad, so I did it.

He wiggled, squirmed, and finally yanked my hands from his pants. Then he looked at me with disgust and pushed me away from him.

I had done what he asked, so why was he mad?

Mama was gone a lot these days and left me home alone.

Now that we'd moved, it wasn't the people in white who came while Mama was gone. It was cousin Mason.

Mama said it was ok to let him in. And just as I came to rely on the people in white for attention, I began to rely on my cousin for his attention.

His visits were frequent but short. He came over, ate, or drank from our refrigerator and made me do what he wanted.

I didn't want to do it. Well, maybe I did, but only because, for a brief while, someone wanted to touch me. Cousin Mason was always nice when he arrived. But after I did what he wanted, he hated me and left without saying a word.

He never said not to tell, but somehow, I just knew I shouldn't. There were always things I couldn't tell Mama.

Sometimes when my cousin came over, Mama was home.

"Hey Auntie," Mason said.

"Hey Mason," Mama said. "Where yo mama?"

"She at home," Mason said.

"What you doing in town?" Mama asked.

"I'm playing in the game tonight," Mason said. "It will be late when it's over, so I was wondering if I could spend the night here."

I smiled. Just like Mama had taught me. But inside, my body was screaming. My palms began to sweat, and I felt like I was going to throw up.

Why was Mama allowing him to stay here overnight? Oh, she doesn't know what he does to me.

"I'm about to wash some clothes," Mama told Mason. "Get Iris to get you something to eat before you leave for the game."

Mama went to the back porch to wash our clothes. When the load was ready to hang on the line, she carried her big basket outside.

Mason had been pretending to read.

"Come here," he called to me.

I went over to where he was sitting on the couch. We could see Mama in the backyard hanging clothes on the line.

I stood there waiting for him to open his pants. But this time, he reached up and touched me between my legs.

This was different, and it startled me. I stepped back.

"Don't do that," Mason commanded. "Come here."

I stepped toward him. He turned his head toward the window and watched Mama hanging clothes. He put one hand down his pants and the other down my shorts.

I could hear him breathing hard. I wanted to run, but I was scared, so I stood there.

Soon he yanked his hands from my pants and his and ran out of the room to the woods behind our house.

I looked out the window and saw Mama hanging clothes on the line. Her basket was now almost empty.

I sat down on the couch and stared at the white wall behind the TV.

"Where's Mason?" Mama asked when she came back inside.

I hadn't heard her come into the room. She startled me, and I gasped.

"What you holling like a fool for?" Mama asked.

"No reason," I said.

Mama looked at me, but it was clear she didn't see me.

I was sure that my face was blank and empty like the wall I stared at so much.

Finally, cousin Mason came back.

"Auntie, you need my help draining the washing machine?" he asked sweetly.

"Yes Mason," Mama said. "That's so nice of you."

Mama walked back out of the room. Mason looked at me and put a finger up to his lips.

Somehow, I knew better than to talk.

Mason made it a habit coming to our home. Sometimes Mama was home when he violated me, but mostly, she wasn't.

The more it happened, the more confused I became. It felt good, but it didn't feel good at all.

My body and my mind were at war with each other. I felt so dirty. I hated going to church. I missed Mr. Jack, and I missed the people who wore white.

My breasts began to grow, and Mama made sure to embarrass me about it in front of cousin Mason.

"She thinks she something now Mason," Mama said. "She budding."

She and Mason laughed. When she turned her head, he winked at me.

Later when he was sucking on my budding breasts, fingering me between my legs, and squirming with his hands inside his pants, he wasn't laughing.

Cousin Mason never went further than touching me. I never resisted. I had grown to look forward to the attention.

I struggled with my feelings.

I wanted Mama to put a stop to it, but once again Mama wasn't there.

Her absence became a pattern. When I needed her most, she was never around.

Dear Diary,

My Mama doesn't see me.

No one does.

Iris

Chapter Seven

'First Times'

Benny Pete

Like most kids, my teenage years were turbulent.

The year I turned 13, Cousin Mason graduated from high school and moved up north. I was happy to see him go. I wanted to be a normal kid.

Mama and me moved into a very nice house in an area of town known as Sand Road. It had indoor plumbing, and I even had my own room again.

That fall when school started, I met the Panes. They lived up the road from us. Mama was friends with Mrs. MayElla and her husband, Mr. Buddy Joe.

The Panes had a lot of kids like Mama and Ms. Helene. I became friends with the girls, and we would play together at my house or sometimes at their house.

Their brother Benny Pete was four years older than me and a junior in high school. Benny Pete was in my band class. He and his best friend, D.J., would tease me and my friend, Puddin. I hated being teased.

On the bus ride home, I always sat in the front while Benny Pete and D.J. sat in the middle. Although I heard him talking about me to his friend D.J., I pretended I didn't.

"Man, what you think she up there thinking?" Benny Pete said to D.J.

"She stuck up," D.J. responded. "Who knows what stuck up girls think about."

I continued to ignore them.

Benny Pete started throwing paper balls at me, and finally, I was forced to respond.

"Stop doing that," I yelled. "Why don't you act your age?"

I was surprised that I was able to stand up for myself. Even in anger, talking to him came naturally.

After a few weeks of him throwing paper balls and me fussing at him to stop, he finally did. He started passing notes. And then we started talking.

Benny Pete was the first person I was able to talk to about how I felt since Mr. Jack died. We talked about everything, and I didn't have to let him touch me in private places for him to pay attention to me. He seemed to genuinely care about me as a person.

Eventually, talking led to kissing and kissing led to touching. After all the physical contact with cousin Mason, I didn't want that with Benny Pete. I didn't want that with anyone. It made me feel bad. I was able to tell him no. And even though I didn't tell him why I didn't want to be intimate, he kept talking to me. That made me happy.

Over time, our conversations made us friends and from friends, we fell in love. I told him everything, and he told me everything.

I was head over heels in love.

On Friday nights, Mama let me go uptown to the football games. Benny Pete and I would leave the game early and walk around town holding hands, talking, and kissing. We never went any further than kissing, but for me, that was more than enough.

I felt so safe with him. We made plans for our future. We would move away from Holly Grove, get married, and have children. We even named our children.

I couldn't get enough of him. He let me wear his watch, and when I was in bed, I'd hold it close to me and dream of our life together.

Normally, I'd take off his watch before I got home and put it inside of my bookbag. I knew Mama would be furious about me having a boyfriend, especially one so much older than me.

This particular time, I forgot. Mama saw it, and hell broke loose.

"Whose watch is that?" Mama yelled.

"Benny Pete Pane," I responded.

"That boy down the road?" Mama asked.

"Yes ma'am," I said.

"He's too old for you," Mama said.

"He loves me," I said. "And I love him."

"I don't care about no love," Mama said. "Give him the watch back. You not seeing him no more. He too old for you. A boy that age only wants one thing from you."

Was Mama right? She did know everything.

But I was in love. Benny Pete wasn't pressuring me about sex. Benny Pete was the only person in my life who gave me hugs and told me he loved me. I couldn't end it with him. For the first time in my life, I was outright disobedient and continued to see him.

One of the downfalls to living in a small town is that nothing is ever secret.

"Helene said she saw you with that boy Friday night," Mama confronted me. "I told you to stop seeing him."

There was nothing I could say. I had no intention of ending the relationship with Benny Pete so I didn't bother to lie and say I would.

By the end of the school year, all of our belongings were packed up in a U-Haul. Mama was moving us to St. Louis.

I was heartbroken. Benny Pete said he was too.

He began to pull away from me. I would see him walking past our house to our neighbor's house. He was friends with a girl down there. I was hurt and afraid.

Would anyone ever love me again?

"Why do you go down to Dora Kellogg's house?" I asked him.

"She's my friend," Benny Pete said sadly. "You're leaving. I'm sad and need someone to talk to about it."

"Why can't you talk to me about how you're feeling?" I hated that the two of them were friends.

"Because your mother doesn't want you to talk to me," Benny Pete said. "Don't you remember that?"

Even though he knew I didn't like it, Benny Pete walked past my house every day after school to go to Pepper's house. I watched him and felt like someone was ripping my heart out.

But what could I do? Mama wouldn't change her mind, and neither would he.

I felt powerless, alone, and so hurt. I was also very angry with Mama. It felt like she was ruining my life. Benny Pete and I had plans beyond high school.

Who else would want to marry me?

We left Holly Grove and moved to St. Louis.

I was traumatized. Everything I'd ever loved was left behind. My friends. Memories of Mr. Jack. And now my first love.

Eddie Carlson

For the next year and a half, Benny Pete and I wrote to each other, but it wasn't the same. All I could think about was that he was there with Pepper, and I was here all alone. Eventually, he graduated high school and his letters stopped coming. I imagined he fell in love with someone else, possibly Pepper, and moved on with his life.

Did he and Pepper have the wedding that we talked about?

Did they name their children the names we'd picked out for our children? Did the home they lived in resemble the home we'd dreamed of buying?

Ms. Helene's daughter, Carol Anne, wrote to me and told me that one of the most popular guys in school asked about me and wanted to know if I'd "give him a chance." (That was how the boys asked girls to be their girlfriend.)

I was thrilled that someone so popular was interested in a nerd like me.

Eddie started writing me letters, and to my surprise, Mama let me go back to Holly Grove for winter break in February of 1985.

I saw Benny Pete, and he seemed interested in talking with me.

But it was too late. I couldn't forget that he'd hurt me and when

I'd wanted us to talk, he had chosen to talk to Pepper.

Besides, I was more interested in seeing Eddie. Eddie was new and he hadn't broken my heart. Benny Pete was old and had let me down. I no longer trusted him.

> Dear Diary,
>
> Mr. Jack left and took all the love in the world with him. I'm alone.
>
> Iris

Mama didn't come to Holly Grove and for the first time in my life, I felt free to do whatever I wanted to do. And what I wanted to do was be with Eddie.

Eddie left word with Carol Anne that he wanted me to come to his house. So, I did.

Eddie's house was dark, hot, and smelled of soiled clothes. There were roaches, too. None of that mattered to me because all I could think of was how lucky I was to be with him. I knew he wanted to have sex, and I was willing. Not because I wanted to, but because to me, it meant I'd be kissed and hugged and loved. I would have a boyfriend again.

But nothing was further from the truth.

Eddie treated me the same as cousin Mason had. He was nice until the sex was over. Then he wanted me to leave.

There were no kisses or hugs and he didn't tell me he loved me.

I couldn't believe that my first time had been so cold and had nothing to do with love. Immediately a wave of regret washed over me. I had made a horrible mistake.

I sat there waiting and hoping he'd have something good to say to me. But he sat there staring at the TV as if I wasn't even there.

It felt worse than what cousin Mason had done. I felt like trash.

I felt like crying, but I didn't.

Even in the dark, I recognized the white wall, blank, spacious, and empty.

The first time I fell in love and the first time I had sex happened on two separate occasions with two different people. Yet, both experiences left me feeling the same way.

Empty.

Chapter Eight

'Where Is My Mama?'

Dr. Onuke was the first black doctor I'd seen.

"My name is Dr. Onuke," he said with a thick African accent. "I'm going to examine you today."

Dr. Onuke smelled of Old Spice cologne, fried chicken, and sweat. The combination wasn't pleasant, and immediately, my stomach began to quiver. Luckily, I hadn't eaten anything, so I was safe from throwing up.

But I hadn't been so lucky in prior weeks. It seems I had always been nauseous. But that was probably because Mama insisted on frying chicken every day.

One day, Mama said I had to go to the doctor.

"We gon see what all this throwing up is about," she said walking fast. I nearly had to run to keep up with her after we got off the bus.

Living in St. Louis had been far from a blessing. The house we lived in was worse than the one we'd left in Arkansas. Again, we had no indoor plumbing. I had my own room, but it was scary. The wallpaper was peeling and there were holes in the ceiling and floors. I was too scared most nights to go to sleep.

Finally, we moved, but this time to a shotgun house a few blocks away. I'd always thought that city-living was far superior to country living. But I was wrong.

This time we moved to a four-family duplex close to downtown St. Louis. I was afraid to be there without Mama, but she never hesitated to leave me home alone.

There was always someone sitting on the stoop, drinking, smoking, and cursing. Sometimes they got really loud, and other times it was so bad, the police were called.

"Maybeline," Uncle Junebug yelled outside our door. "Open up, girl and let yo brother in."

I loved Uncle Junebug. He was old and skinny and smelled like alcohol all the time, but he was kind, and he made me laugh. He was another adult who took the time to smile and talk to me like Mr. Jack did.

"Mama ain't home, Uncle Junebug," I yelled through the screen door. "She went to the welfare office."

"Alright then, baby girl. I'll see her when she gets back."

I had learned my lesson about letting people in when Mama wasn't home. Not even Uncle Junebug could be trusted as far as I was concerned.

Our shotgun house was small. The living room was the first room from the front door, then my bedroom and next, the kitchen. Our bathroom was right off from the bedroom before you got to the kitchen.

Mama slept on the couch, and I slept in the bed. It was my idea to put the dresser in the kitchen and use it as a buffet because there was no room for it in the bedroom. We didn't have a dining room table, so it worked.

Mama frying chicken so close to my bedroom was no wonder I was so nauseous and sick. The smell of Crisco and greens every day would make anyone sick.

Right?

I was hoping Dr. Onuke could talk sense into her. I'd tried to tell her what the Home Economics teacher from my new school had told us about fried foods, but Mama wasn't trying to hear it.

"Gal, ain't nothing no white woman can tell me about cooking!"

I watched Dr. Onuke walk down to the end of the table where I was already in a gown and in stirrups.

Mama made me wear a dress today. It was a sleeveless pink dress with white, thick vertical stripes. The matching jacket gave it a more grown-up look, and I wore white sandals that had gotten scuffed up but were still presentable. I felt pretty.

We still didn't have a car, so we walked everywhere or rode the bus. It was hard to keep white shoes clean when you walked so much.

"I will exam you now. I need to feel for your uterus." Dr. Onuke said to me.

I didn't know what that meant so I said nothing. I felt his fingers inside of me. Then I heard him moan.

"You are now going to feel some pressure, but don't be alarmed."

Dr. Onuke was standing very close to my bottom. I felt the pressure I'd been warned about. It felt familiar and unwanted. I wanted to cry out, but I didn't. I knew this wasn't right. I looked around the room, but there was no one there to help me.

I turned my head and there was my friend, the white wall. I focused on it and willed myself to disappear.

It was an odd thing that Dr. Onuke's walls here in downtown St. Louis, Dr. Buckhead's walls in Clarendon, and the walls in our old country home were all white, empty, cold, and bare.

There was nothing there to see or feel.

I'll never escape the white wall, I thought.

"Ah, my dear," Dr. Onuke's African Accent pulled me back into reality. "You are nearly three months along."

Suddenly all emotions and feelings left my body. I just lay there with my dress up, my legs spread wide in stirrups, and my heart smashed beyond recognition.

What had just happened? What did he say and what does that mean? Three months to what?

Dr. Onuke went to the sink and washed his ungloved hands. I continued to lay there and stared now at the back of his head.

He needed a haircut.

I needed my Mama.

Then the nurse came in.

"You can sit up now," she said sweetly. "Your exam is over."

I couldn't figure out how to get my legs from the stirrups. The room was freezing, and I began to shake.

"Miss Williams, are you ok?" The nurse asked as she hurriedly began preparing the room for the next patient.

I shook my head no, but she wasn't looking. Finally, I freed my legs from the stirrups and began to get dressed.

Where is my Mama?

"Is my Mama here?" I asked softly. The tears were threatening to fall, but I didn't dare allow them the satisfaction.

I wish Mr. Jack was here. He'd know what to do. He'd hold me until I wasn't scared. He'd explain to me why all of this was happening, and he'd reassure me that everything was going to be alright.

But he wasn't here. And he wasn't coming back.

"She's in the waiting area." The nurse reported without looking at me. "Now that you're dressed, step outside to see the receptionist about your next appointment."

My next appointment. Why did I need to come back? What was going on? Where was my Mama? Why did she leave me here alone?

It seemed every time something bad happened to me, I was always left alone to fend for myself. This was one of those times where I knew I had to be strong and tough it out. No one was coming to rescue me like in the books I read.

There would be no prince or knight on a white horse to carry me away from my problems. It was just me and only me. I mustered up the strength and decided to face what lay ahead.

After dressing, I stepped out of the exam room and walked over to the receptionist area. The room was full of waiting patients now. She handed me a plastic bag.

"Dr. Onuke will want to see you again in one month," She said without emotion.

I took the appointment card and headed out toward the waiting area. It seemed as though all eyes were on me. I felt a terrible sense of embarrassment wash over me.

I scanned the room for Mama. The crowd seemed to be staring at the bag I held, so I looked down at it too.

On the outside of the bag was the picture of a baby wearing only it's pamper. It was smiling a toothless grin and holding a bottle of milk.

I looked back up in time to see Mama. She looked at the bag and back up at me.

I saw the anger in her eyes. I hung my head down in defeat and instinctively, held the bag to my stomach.

Mama got up and walked past me out of the doctor's office.

Dear Diary,

I'm having a baby!

I have no idea what it means or what to expect. I'm terrified of what's going to happen.

Mama is very mad at me.

I hear her on the phone telling everyone how dumb I am and how she ain't lifting a finger to do nothing.

She's right. It was dumb of me to trust Eddie.

But what do I do now?

Iris

Iris M. Williams

As I saw the door close behind her, I wondered how I was ever going to make it through this.

Where was my Mama?

Chapter Nine

'I'm Having a Baby'

Mama didn't talk to me for days after the doctor's appointment.

It hurt, but by then I'd learned how to deal with it. I kept quiet and to myself. I stayed in my room even more and because I had morning sickness so much, I rarely ate.

She tried to make me, but it didn't do any good. It would just come right back up.

Having a baby was something I never even considered as part of my reality. I didn't know how to process the information. I didn't know how I was supposed to feel.

To be happy somehow felt like going against what Mama wanted for me.

The silent treatment lasted for days.

As bad as the silent treatment was, I can't say that talking was any better. The angry, hateful words stung like a bee. And afterward, there was no salve to soothe the pain.

I was a sophomore in high school. How was this going to work?

Mama insisted I drop out. She said riding the bus would injure the baby.

"All that jarring ain't good," she said with finality. "You'll just have to quit."

Again, my heart was crushed. All I had in life were books and learning. What would I do with a baby? I had nothing to give it. I wasn't even sure I would love it. Was I capable of loving? Was anyone capable of loving me?

Days turned into weeks and weeks into months. I festered in unanswered questions and uncertainty.

How would I care for a baby? I didn't have any money. I didn't know what to do. I'd never changed a diaper. Since I wasn't in school, I had no access to books or information.

Mama and I didn't talk about anything.

She spent her time on the phone with her friends, mostly pretending I wasn't there.

For months, I sat in a chair and worried about the future.

Would I ever go back to school?

So, I just sat in the chair, ate cereal, drank orange juice, watched TV, and waited for my life to change.

Then one day, Mama broke the silence.

"Whose the baby daddy?" She was just as angry as she was the day we found out I was pregnant.

I didn't want to answer her. But I was too scared not to. I wanted to lie, but I knew better.

"Eddie Carlson," I said softly. I didn't dare look up at her.

"Who his peoples?"

"His mama is named May Rose," I said, again avoiding Mama's eyes.

"Does he know?"

"Yes," I said wishing I were any place but here.

"What he say?"

"He said it's not his," I said willing the tears not to fall.

"Well," Mama said. "Is it?"

It hurt bad enough that he didn't believe me, but to have Mama question me cut deeper. Maybe he wasn't such a bad person after all. I mean if my own mother didn't believe me, why should he?

"Yes, it's his."

Truth is, Eddie's refusal to believe my baby was his baby had really shaken me up. I knew he was my first. Well, he was the first that I remembered, anyway.

I thought back to what Dr. Buckhead said so many years ago. Maybe Eddie wasn't my first, but this baby was definitely his.

"Well, now we gotta figure out how to get the things the baby will need."

"Yes ma'am," I said and was immediately filled with guilt.

Mama didn't work, and we were on a fixed income. Another mouth to feed and clothe was going to be an added burden for her. I was only 15, and according to her, my hip was too raggedy to work.

I felt so horrible. Not only was my education affected, but I was also now contributing to Mama's stress.

How could I have been so stupid to think that someone like Eddie would actually care about someone like me?

I was convinced that if there was a bad choice to be made, I would make it.

Right now, though, there was no choice. I was having a baby.

Dear Diary,

I want a love of my own.

I know I have a baby now, but maybe someone will find me valuable enough to love and to marry.

Mama says she is leaving with my baby girl so I will be all alone.

I hope I find someone soon.

Iris

Chapter Ten

'A Ticking Time Bomb'

I had my baby in the winter of 1985 and Mama moved us back to Arkansas, this time to Little Rock. I made it back to school just in time to finish up my junior year of high school at Parkview.

Luckily, I had taken most of the courses I needed to graduate, so even though I missed a whole semester of school, I would still graduate on time.

Mama bonded with my baby girl, and that took some of the stress off me. I was so worried she'd be mean to her, too. But she adored my daughter and pushed her way into the role of mother. They often traveled without me and I was left home alone.

Being alone was harder to forget than what I'd been through with Benny Pete and Eddie. So, it wasn't long before I was making bad choices again.

I met Monty the summer before I graduated from high school. He was from Stamps, Arkansas. He reminded me a lot of the lead singer from the group, Atlantic Starr. Monty had a way with words and charmed me right out of my underwear. No matter, I'd sworn off guys since having a baby at 16 with a guy who refused to believe it was his.

Our relationship was a whirlwind. I knew I was in love. The first chance I got to be alone with him, I took it. He'd been telling me how much he loved me pretty much since the day we met, so I didn't think anything of having sex with him. After all, I was practically grown.

In my mind, we would get married, have a family, and live happily ever after.

Again, I was wrong.

When the summer was over, Monty left with a promise to return but months later, when there hadn't been any calls or letters, old hurts resurfaced, and it was Benny Pete all over again.

I lay in bed crying my eyes out and literally made myself sick. The nausea was overwhelming and that's when I realized what was happening.

No, not again!

But it was true. I was pregnant again. I was alone again.

Mama had always told me I was an ignorant ass fool, and now more than ever, I was convinced she was right.

Why did I let this happen again?

Only God knew the thoughts that were surfacing in my mind. I desperately wanted to talk to my Mama. But I knew she wouldn't listen, and I was certain she wouldn't understand.

Turns out, Mama knew more than I gave her credit.

"We are moving back to St. Louis," Mama announced.

I didn't want to go back to St. Louis. The place held bad memories for me, and it just wasn't a place I could call home.

"But I don't want to go," I responded.

"I don't mean you," Mama said. "Me and the baby are moving."

"But I have a full scholarship to UALR," I said sadly. "What will I do?"

"I guess you better take it," Mama said matter-of-factly.

I didn't know what any of that meant.

Did she have a right to take my baby? Why didn't she care about my education? Even if I insisted on taking my baby, how would I raise her?

I had nothing and no one.

Was St. Louis an option? Mama said her plans didn't include me.

And what about this new situation I was in? How would I tell Mama about that? What would she do?

"We are going to find you an apartment next week," Mama said. "I'm having your disability check signed over to you."

Mama had already figured everything out. She found me an apartment across the street from the college and had my disability check turned over to me. She rented a U-Haul truck, moved my bedroom furniture, and TV to the new apartment. Then took my baby and left the state.

I was indeed pregnant. And I'm certain Mama knew before I did. After all, she was the one who was buying my sanitary napkins.

I didn't know what to do or who to turn to for help. I woke up each day and just did what I had to do. I went to school, did my homework, ate, and went to bed only to do it all over again the next day.

My freshman year of college, my grades soared – all A's the first semester. I declined parties and social situations. Right after class, I came home to study.

However, by the second semester, my mind was no longer focused on school, but on my growing belly.

I would have to make a decision soon. I couldn't put it off much longer.

I'd gained quite a bit of weight after Mr. Jack died. By the time I hit puberty, I was officially plus-sized. So, hiding a pregnancy wasn't a big deal. Actually, I lost weight.

My body actually didn't betray me for once.

Dear Diary,

I'm not a strong person.

All I do is make mistakes.

Iris

Iris M. Williams

Physically, I was fine, but emotionally I was a ticking time bomb.

Chapter Eleven

'A Reprieve'

The apartment Mama left me in was actually a three-bedroom apartment that the landlord rented to three different tenants. Our bedrooms were private, but we were to share the kitchen and one bathroom.

It was horrible.

I'm pretty sure that I'm a germaphobe, but my living conditions up to that point never fully allowed me to be one. I mean, living in a place without indoor plumbing, how particular can you really be?

The bathroom experience was so traumatizing, I still don't remember much about it.

However, the kitchen caused me to nearly get evicted.

My room was the first of the three rooms to be rented and for a while, I was the only one there. I was scared most nights to go to sleep or come home after dark, but I managed.

Then the lady with the big wig moved in. She looked strange and behaved just as strange.

I was on a fixed income and only got $33 in food stamps a month. After paying my rent, I really didn't have much disposable income, so every dollar counted. Mama had taught me how to budget and shop accordingly, so I used the $33 to purchase meats and staple items. For the first few months, I did well. The food lasted me through the month.

However, when the lady with the big wig moved in, I began to run out of food.

There were days I went without eating. It was so hard to go to school and walk through the cafeteria smelling food that I knew I couldn't afford.

I knew I wasn't eating my food and I couldn't imagine someone would steal from me – least of all a grown person, but that was exactly what was happening.

The lady with the big wig was stealing my food. I couldn't prove it, but it was the only logical explanation. No one else had a key but the two of us.

I decided I'd talk to the landlord about it.

"Well, she reported that you were stealing her food," he said with a chuckle.

"What," I said, shocked. "No sir, that's not true. I never even see her buy any food."

"Do you have proof?" He wanted to know.

"No," I said slowly.

"Then there is nothing I can do," he said, and his disinterest was evident.

I left feeling worse than I did before I talked to him. It was one thing for her to be stealing, but now she had him believing I was a thief.

What was I going to do?

Finally, I let go of my pride and talked to my sister, Lola, about it.

Lola was 20 years older than me. She lived in Little Rock with her two daughters.

"Hi," I said. "How are you?"

"I'm ok, lil sis," she said but sounded anything but ok.

"What's wrong?"

"Nothing. Just tired and hurting."

"Well, I'm sorry to hear that." And then I lost my nerve. "I was just calling to say hey."

"I'm glad you called," she said. "Don't you want to let your nieces come stay the weekend with you?"

"Sure," I said and meant it. It was lonely there all by myself. "But my place is very small, and I don't have much food."

"Oh, it'll be ok. They don't care. As long as you got a TV, they'll be alright. And I'll bring you some food."

She brought them over and what was supposed to be for the weekend, became an every week arrangement. Turns out my apartment was closer to their school. We were cramped, but we didn't mind. It felt like a slumber party and I was so glad not to be alone.

At first, I was afraid my secret would be exposed. But again, I was a big girl and no one ever paid me much attention, so it all worked out.

The girls stayed with me for a few months and then my sister decided I should come live with them.

"You'll have your own room," she said. "I know y'all tired of being so cramped."

"We don't mind it so much," I said.

"Well, actually it would help me out," Lola confessed. "Maureen left without notice, so I need a roommate to help me with the rent. You can just pay me what you're paying."

So, I agreed and moved in with her and her girls. I have to admit it felt good to be in a home again. My apartment had begun to feel like a closet.

During the day, I went to school and then walked home with the girls. We came home and fixed dinner, ate, watched TV, and laughed until it was time for bed.

Lola worked and then every day after work, she went to happy hour. We didn't mind being left home alone. The three of us talked, laughed, watched TV, and did our homework.

We all settled into a routine and for a while, I forgot all about the fact that I was having a baby.

Dear Diary

I'm going to live with my sister. I hope I can still keep my secret.

Iris,

Chapter Twelve

'An Answered Prayer'

Now that I look back on it, meeting Ansha Harris wasn't a coincidence after all.

For weeks, I'd been walking the same way home, but this particular day is when I noticed the huge billboard:

Pregnant? Scared? Let us help you.

Catholic Diocese of Little Rock

501-221-0070

I made it home before anyone else got there and I hesitantly dialed the number. The voice on the other end was soft and right away, I felt at ease.

"Hi," I said in a small voice. "I need to speak to someone about adoption."

"Hello," the sweet voice said. "My name is Ansha, and I'm a social worker specializing in adoption. What is your name?"

"My name is Iris," I said.

"Nice to meet you, Iris," Ansha said. "How far along are you?"

"I don't know," I said and was suddenly embarrassed and afraid.

"That's ok," Ansha said. "Have you seen a doctor?"

"No," I said.

"Well, would you like to meet with me to talk in person?" Ansha asked. "We can meet at Wendy's, and I'll buy you lunch."

Wendy's sounded delicious. These days, I was always hungry, so I quickly agreed. I figured even if she couldn't help me, at least I'd get a good meal.

I met with Ansha and while I ate, she explained the adoption process. It wasn't the choice I wanted to make, but rather the choice I had to make. I had no money to keep the baby or get rid of it. Honestly, as terrified as I was of an abortion, if I had the money, I probably would have done it. I wanted my life back.

Ansha not only paid for our meal, but she also scheduled a visit to the doctor. I told her I didn't have any money, but she assured me none of this would cost me anything. She said the church would pay for all of my expenses.

My appointment was in the Doctor's building on University. When the nurse called my name, I was surprised to see Ansha stand up too.

"I can go with you if you want me to," she said, and I knew she meant it.

I nodded. Mama had not gone into my doctor's appointments with me. I was happy I wouldn't be alone. I was afraid of what may happen.

I got a glimpse of the doctor as I waited in the waiting room. He was speaking to one of the nurses.

The doctor was white and slim, but my mind quickly went back to Dr. Buckhead and I got really nervous.

The nurse called my name and I panicked. "Maybe this isn't a good idea," I said to Ansha.

"Oh, dear one, there is nothing to be afraid of. I'm right here with you. We need to make sure that you're healthy and that the baby is healthy, too. Is that ok?"

I wanted the baby to be ok, so I nodded my head and let her lead me to the exam room.

The room was full of people. Besides me, there was Ansha, the nurse, and Dr. Benford. I began to relax.

"Looks like you are indeed pregnant," Dr. Benford said. "Your due date is December 25."

"A Christmas baby," Ansha said with excitement.

I smiled with her, but I couldn't be happy.

"And it seems like you and the baby are doing just fine." Dr. Benford said. "I see no abnormalities and the heartbeat is strong."

I was grateful. Maybe now I could sleep since I'd stumbled upon a solution to my problem.

After the appointment, Ansha took me for a meal again.

"So, what does your family think about your choice for adoption," Ansha asked.

"They don't know," I responded.

"When will you tell them?" She asked.

"I don't plan to," I said.

"But won't they wonder where the baby went?"

"They don't know I'm pregnant," I said.

She looked at me with a puzzled expression. I knew what she was thinking.

"I'm invisible in my family," I said without emotion. "No one has noticed."

"Well, I'm sure that isn't true," Ansha said, "But I'm here and I notice you. I think you're brave and from our brief encounter, you're smart too. You're giving your child a good start and, in the process, you're going to make some parents very happy."

I hadn't thought that far.

I'd only thought about what this adoption meant for me. It meant getting my freedom back and having a chance at a life again.

Would I really be able to walk away from my baby? Could I give it to strangers? Would they be good to my baby? Would my baby grow up to hate me?

Iris M. Williams

I had thousands of questions and no answers.

I went to bed with doubts and woke up with fears.

And then the time came.

Ansha and I had rehearsed the routine. We'd already gone to the hospital to pre-register. I was to call her when I went into labor and she'd come right away to get me.

It was a good plan, but things didn't work out that way.

Around 7 on a Thursday evening, I felt sharp pains. I'd been through this before, so I knew what was happening.

I panicked.

Ansha and I didn't discuss what to do if it were evening.

Everyone was at home. I couldn't just leave. What would I tell them? Where would I say I was going? I had to stay in the hospital for at least three days. Where would I tell Lola and the girls I was?

Overcome with fear and shame, I put on my nightgown and got into bed.

Dear Diary,

I just want to be loved.

Iris

"Iris," Lola knocked on the door and walked inside. "Aren't you going to eat dinner?"

"No," I said. "I don't feel good. I think I'm just going to go to sleep."

"Do you need some medicine?"

"No," I'll be fine. "I just need to rest."

"Well ok," she said. "I'll check on you in the morning."

I tossed and turned all night. The pains were coming so fast and hard, I could hardly catch my breath. I wanted to scream. I wanted to cry. But I held it all in.

Finally, morning came, and everyone left.

I waited a few minutes and then I dialed Ansha's number.

"Ansha," I said holding back tears. "I think I need to get to the hospital. I think the baby is coming."

"Ok, let's stay calm," Ansha said but she sounded just as nervous as I felt. "I need to drop my daughter off at school first. Is that going to be ok?"

I felt pressure between my legs.

"Um, no I really think I need to get there now."

"Oh dear," Ansha said now in full panic mode. "I'll be right there."

And she did. Not ten minutes later, she arrived, and I walked out to her car.

She drove as fast as she could, and we made it to the hospital in record time. Luckily, we were only minutes away from Doctor's Hospital on University.

I somehow managed to walk to the front doors of the hospital and a nurse saw my face and came out with a wheelchair.

They wheeled me to the front desk, put a band on my arm (thank God we'd already pre-registered), and took me right to an exam room.

As I got up to lay on the table, I felt like I had to have a bowel movement.

"I think the baby is coming now," I said with wide eyes.

"Now?" both the nurse and Ansha said.

I had managed to put on jeans and as they both pulled on a leg of my pants, I began pushing.

Iris M. Williams

The baby was about to be born.

Epilogue

'The Choices We Make'

Mama had been telling me my whole life that I was ignorant and now finally I saw what she saw.

With so many bad choices under my belt, it was clear that I was dumb. I had to be to make so many bad choices.

When Mr. Jack died, so did a part of me.

The little girl who laughed and talked and dreamed was silenced and in her place was the girl with the sad eyes.

Who would be there for her? Who would fight for her? Who would listen to her? Who would care?

Mama was not there.

Reverend Dover talked about God and faith, but I couldn't see either in my life. Maybe God died with Mr. Jack.

The people I relied on were gone or they let me down.

It was clear that I had to get smart because the only person I could count on was me.

My faith was in myself.

Book II
Faith In No One

For the little girl with sad eyes ...

"I could have freed a thousand more slaves if only they'd known they were slaves."

Harriett Tubman

Foreword

I think the formation of my prison began with the death of my father, Mr. Jack when I was six. That was a time of turmoil and confusion. Mr. Jack left and took his love with him. And I was left to search for his replacement.

Can love be replaced?

When I first read the quote from Harriett Tubman, it was startling to me. How could people NOT know they were slaves? Then it dawned on me; slavery isn't just a physical state; it can also be an emotional one.

For years, I lived captive in a state of mind created by Mama. In that world, I wasn't good enough, deserving, or capable.

I imagine the people Harriet tried to help refused her assistance. I can imagine this because as I look back over my life, I see that help was there for me, but I didn't know I needed it. Like many I said, "This is just who I am."

When I left Mama's house, I thought that was my freedom. And so, I lived my life with a false sense of freedom – doing what I wanted, or more accurate, doing what others wanted me to do.

That wasn't true freedom.

It can be said that prior to leaving Mama's house, things happened to me. But once I left her home, I had control over my life – to some degree. But because I didn't' recognize I was a prisoner of my past; I couldn't see that I had options.

For years I wandered around searching for something that I already possessed. I thought it was the love of my father. I thought it was the love of Mama. I thought it was the love of a man.

Finally, I realized that the love I'd been longing for was my own.

You can't change what you don't acknowledge.

The R&B Group, En Vogue said, "Free your mind, and the rest will follow."

I agree.

When I finally realized that it was me who needed to love me, I could begin the tough work of first discovering who I was.

Knowing who you are is the first step in learning to love who you are. Yes, there were things about me that I didn't like. Some of those things I could change and others I had to grow to appreciate.

In the end, the effort was worth it. I was worth it.

Acknowledgment

To God, be the glory.

Prologue

I couldn't sleep.

The pain was bad, but not unbearable. I knew what was happening. I'd done this before. This time, there would be no rush of activity. This pregnancy had been a secret to everyone except Ansha, the social worker handling the adoption. I decided to wait until morning to call. I didn't want to wake her.

Also, what would I tell Lola?

I tossed and turned the whole night. My mind was wandering from one thought to the next. I didn't know if I would be able to hold the baby inside of me until morning.

Somehow, I did, and by the time Ansha came to get me, I was on the verge of giving birth. Luckily, we had already pre-registered at the hospital.

"Ansha," I said, sounding calmer than I felt. "Can you come to get me? I think the baby is coming."

"Oh my," she said with alarm. "Do I have time to drop my daughter off?"

I said yes but felt I should have said no. I didn't want to be a bother.

"Don't be worrisome," Mama had said.

While I waited, I worked hard to quiet the thoughts in my head.

What would Mama think about this?

Ansha arrived, and we got to University Hospital quickly. The nurses wheeled me into the exam room. I think Ansha must have called ahead to alert them we were coming because they were outside waiting for us.

There was no time to take my jeans off me. The nurse cut them. I felt the urge to push. In what seemed like seconds, the baby was born.

Christmas, 1987, I pushed my baby boy out of my womb and tried to push aside any feelings of love I had for him. I knew I couldn't keep him.

There had been time for drugs this time, so the birth was considered natural. But what I was about to do wasn't natural at all.

What kind of person gives their baby away to a stranger?

Winter and Christmas would never be the same.

Introduction

'DeJa Vu'

When it was all over, I was taken to a room on a regular floor. Ansha thought it was best not to be on the maternity ward since I wasn't keeping my baby.

I was in a private room, but I wasn't alone. My friend, the white wall, was back. As usual, his face wasn't pleasant, but it was a familiar sight. I could always count on him showing up. The white wall had been the only consistency in my life. Empty, cold, and depressing, he never changed. Neither had my life

I looked down at my baby boy. He really was beautiful. His eyes were shut tight, and I was hoping he wouldn't open them. I didn't want him to see the person who would give him away. I didn't want him to remember me on those terms. Instead, I hoped he would remember the comfort of my womb and the love I had but hadn't known how to share.

It was a shame I couldn't keep him. His older sister would probably be happy if I could. Of course, she was the only one who would be happy.

Mama would be furious. The little boy's daddy would be furious, if he knew. And I was numb. I was numb because of the guilt, shame, and disappointment.

How could I let this happen again?

I was eighteen and had just given birth to my second child — another baby I couldn't raise. I was barely able to take care of myself. Mama had already taken my baby girl.

Would she even want another child?

The nurse came and interrupted my thoughts. "He is beautiful," she said as she swiftly removed him from my arms. "And has a head full of hair."

I nodded my head, unable to speak. Mama would have yelled at me, "Open your mouth and talk."

"We need to take him for some shots, but we can bring him right back, ok?"

I nodded again as I attempted a weak smile, but it was overpowered by sadness.

Thoughts of my past began to swim throughout my mind, thoughts of defeat, and then my head began to ache from all the voices I heard:

"What's the matter with you," Mama would say, "why you noddin' yo head like a deaf mute?"

"I never agreed to a baby," Monty would have said if he'd bothered to talk to me. I hadn't heard anymore from him since he disappeared.

Mr. Jack would have been devastated. "What have you done, Chick-o-mo-stick?"

I was disappointed. This wasn't what I wanted for my life.

There were always so many questions.

Why was this happening to me? Why couldn't someone love me and stay? What was it about me that caused people to leave?

There were never any answers.

Getting pregnant twice in less than two years was shameful.

What kind of girl allows this to happen?

I'd had dreams. I wanted to go to college to become a nurse or a teacher, to get married, to buy a home, and THEN to have kids. Instead, my dreams turned into a nightmare.

There was a soft knock on the door. It was Ansha.

"Iris," Ansha said as she came to my side. "When I left you were sleeping."

Ansha's free spirit was evident in her appearance. Her flowing tunic and sandals spoke volumes about her persona. I got a faint whiff of her flowery perfume. Her long dark hair nearly reached the tops of her hips.

She leaned over and kissed me on my forehead. Then, she smiled. I knew she approved of my decision, and she didn't judge me. But she was the only one.

What must God think of me?

The nurse returned, placed the baby back into my arms, and left with a knowing glance at Ansha.

"He's so precious," Ansha said. "How are you holding up?"

I wasn't holding up, but I had to be strong and somehow get through it.

"OK," I whispered.

"Are you ready to sign the papers?" Ansha asked. "You have the right to change your mind, you know."

"I'm ready," I said. There was no point in putting it off. There were no alternatives.

Ansha pulled the papers from her briefcase, pushed my uneaten dinner aside, and laid the papers on the food tray. With my baby in my left arm, I signed the papers with my right hand.

"Do you want me to take him now?" Ansha asked.

I nodded my head, yes.

I kissed the top of my baby boy's head, whispered in his ear, and handed him gently to Ansha.

She walked out of the room and took a huge chunk of my heart with her. I turned over on my side, and there was my friend, the white wall.

This time, there was something there.

I blinked several times to get a good look, and that's when it happened.

I'd been moved from the maternity ward. There were no babies on this floor. But I could still hear crying.

Wait, no; the crying I heard was coming from me.

Tears fell from my eyes like rain. I cried for hours as I stared at the white wall.

Mama wasn't here, and neither was Mr. Jack.

So, I didn't have to be a big girl.

Chapter One

'Baby Jamie'

For the entire time I was pregnant, I hadn't wanted to be. It's a horrible thing to say, but it's my truth. I was hoping I'd miscarry.

I wasn't eating properly. I wasn't resting. I wasn't seeing a doctor. Yet, my baby was born strong, healthy, and completely normal.

I had worried about his health and was amazed and grateful he was ok.

I guess he was destined to be born to me.

After having the baby and NOT being pregnant, ironically I found myself wanting to be. When I was pregnant, my baby was with me. I'd felt him move, and although I hadn't realized it, it had become comforting. Someone had been with me. I hadn't been entirely alone.

Now that he was born, I felt empty.

Sitting in that hospital room, I realized I was all alone again. I'd given away more than my flesh and blood, a piece of me was now gone.

I rolled over on my side and looked out the window at the night sky. There was a world out there that my son would be in, and I'd have no access to him. I couldn't call and check on him. I wouldn't hear his voice. I'd never know if he was happy, hurt, or in danger, and I certainly couldn't help him.

Had I done the right thing?

But what choice did I have? How would I feed him? Where would I get pampers from? Where would we live?

What would Mama say? What would Mama do? Would she come to take him too?

I didn't know I was crying again until I realized my pillow was wet. And I willed myself to stop. Maybe all I could do now was be a big girl for Mr. Jack and not cry so much.

The nurse came in and asked if I was in pain.

"Yes," I said, but it wasn't physical.

Ansha had told me that I could write a letter to my son. She said she would give it to his adopted mom, and when he was old enough, his adopted mom would give it to him.

"Would you like something for the pain?" The nurse asked.

"No," I said. I was sure there wasn't anything she could give me to stop my heart from hurting. "But I would like a pen, paper, and an envelope, please."

"Sure, honey," she said sweetly and left the room.

When she returned, she brought the items I'd asked for and some juice.

"I figured you could use something to drink," she said kindly and gave me a sad look.

What did she think of me?

I thanked her, and as soon as she walked out of the room, I began to write:

Jamie,

I don't know if your mother will keep this name for you, but this is the name I chose. I chose it because it is close to the French word, Je'Taime, which means love.

Even though I'm giving you away, it isn't because I don't love you. You're a part of me and always will be.

If you ever want to know why I did this, I want you to know it is because I wasn't strong enough to fight. I'm not very old and not very smart, and so I don't know how to stand up to the things that are standing in the way of me keeping you.

I don't want you to have a hard life. I want you to have a good life. And giving you to someone who wants you and can take care of you seems like the best option.

I do hope that you can forgive me and that you won't hate me. I'll understand if you do. Right now, I hate me. And I wish I were stronger. When you're 18 and if you decide you want to know me, I'd like that very much.

I'll stay in touch with the social worker so she can always know where to find me.

I do love you.

The paper was so wet that some of the words began to smudge. I folded the paper and put it inside the envelope.

I sealed it and kissed the outside of the envelope just as I'd kissed my baby boy's head for the last time.

Would I ever be strong? Would I ever have the courage to live life on my own terms? Would I ever see my baby boy again? Would he hate me?

Each question led me to another until finally, I stopped thinking and focused on not feeling.

I have 18 years to figure it all out, I thought. For now, I need to find peace.

As hard as I tried to focus on the future, I couldn't see one that I liked. I was unsure and unsteady and unprepared. I had no idea what I would do now.

I'd finished the first semester of my freshman year of college. I could go back for the spring semester, but school felt like a complete waste of time now.

What was the point? What kind of life could I possibly have?

Giving my son away was hard for me, but I hoped it would be great for him.

I imagined he'd be placed with a family who was overjoyed at having him. They would have a huge home with a backyard and siblings who were his age so he wouldn't grow up feeling alone. They would love him, kiss him, and tell him how smart he was. They would encourage him to learn and to express his feelings no matter what they were. They would shower him with so much love that sometimes he'd get angry because he would feel he couldn't breathe, which was better than being left in the cold without love.

That dream kept me sane.

I carried many secrets, but this one was the one that threatened to break my back. I longed for someone to confide in.

Years later, I tested the water and tried to tell someone about what I'd done. It hadn't gone well at all.

"What if I told you I gave a baby up for adoption?" I said to him. He was some guy I considered dating.

"I'd say you were a damn fool," he said.

"Why would you say that?" I asked cautiously. "Isn't that better than abortion?"

"Hell, naw," he continued. "Both are just plain stupid, and so are the women who do that shit. But hell, I think women who give up their babies are the worst. How you know that some fool ain't beating or molesting the baby?"

I was crushed. His response told me two things:

One, I couldn't think about my son anymore because my mind would now drift from the happy dreams I'd wished for him, to the harsh realities of the uncertainty in which I'd placed him.

Two, I would never be able to tell anyone what I'd done.

No one could ever possibly understand.

Chapter Two

'Bradford James'

A couple of days passed, and I returned to Lola's house on Sunday. I'd called her from the hospital and told her I'd went to Holly Grove for the weekend and that I'd be back on Sunday. She had simply said, "Ok."

When I returned on Sunday, I slipped into my room, got into bed and pretended to be asleep. No one thought to check on me.

The room felt so empty and cold.

After having my baby and giving it away, it became clear to me that I could no longer stay in Little Rock. Being separated from both of my children became too much to bear. My mind wasn't on school anymore; I flunked out and lost my scholarship.

I got on the Greyhound bus in January of 1988, with only my clothes and headed to Indiana, where Mama and my baby girl were now living. They were both staying with my sister Catherine.

Mama, my baby girl, and I shared a room, but with Mama's attitude, the room was too crowded. I spent most nights on the sofa.

I was near my baby girl, but I was far from being her mother. Mama was her mother, and all I was good for was carrying out her wishes.

"Go to the sto and get some cornmeal so I can make dinner," Mama ordered.

I was eighteen, the mother of two, yet Mama still had no respect for me.

"Yes, ma'am," I said and began the short walk to the 7-11.

On the way, I spotted a tall, dark-skinned guy walking in the same direction.

"You going to the 7-11 too?" He asked and flashed a big toothy grin. It reminded me of Mr. Jack's smile. I liked him.

"Yep," I said and smiled back politely.

"Do you mind if I walk with you?" He asked as he matched his stride with mine.

I shook my head no, but then remembered how Mama hated that. "I don't mind," I said.

We went to the store, and I got the cornmeal for Mama. He bought a red Faygo pop.

"I like those too," I said. "Actually, they're my favorite, but they make me burp."

He laughed, and I did too.

When it was time for me to take the turn back to my sister's apartment, I awkwardly said, "Well, this is where I turn off."

"I can walk you to your place if you want me to," he said, still smiling.

I didn't know what Mama would think of that, but something told me it wasn't a good idea.

"Nah," I said quickly, trying to come up with a believable excuse.

"OK," he said but never stopped smiling. "Maybe next time."

"Maybe," I responded and turned to head back to my sister's apartment. I didn't figure I'd see him again since I wouldn't let him walk me home.

But the next day, I was walking back to the 7-11, and there he was again. At first, I was scared.

Was he stalking me?

I quickly got over it when he smiled and asked if he could walk with me again. I agreed and walking to the 7-11 soon became a daily routine.

Eventually, I agreed to let him walk me home.

"This is Bradford James," I said as we walked into the apartment. "He lives in Brentwood Apartments with his mother and little brother."

"Nice to meet y'all," he said and smiled.

Bradford smiled a lot. In the short time I'd known him, I realized his disposition was unlike any person I'd met. Nothing seemed to bother him, which was good because Mama was very unpredictable.

"Mmmm, hunh," Mama mumbled. "Who yo peoples?"

"Iris, he's nice!" My sister Catherine said before Bradford could answer. "So tall and has such nice teeth. I love a man with a great smile!"

I was mortified at the both of them. Mama was too cold, and Catherine was just too much.

"So, Bradford," Catherine continued with a barrage of questions, "Where do you live? Where do you work? And how did you meet Iris?"

We all laughed. Catherine was known for asking rapid fire questions. Bradford took it all in stride and answered all of her questions; then, she asked another round. But before he could answer, my baby girl came into the room. She was walking now and talking. She was so smart.

"And who is this pretty little thing," Bradford asked. "Iris, is this your niece?"

I hadn't told Bradford that I had a baby or that I'd had two and given one up for adoption.

"No," I said, suddenly afraid of his reaction. "This is my daughter."

"Oh," Bradford said and continued to smile. "I see where she gets her good looks."

I was shocked. No one had called me pretty since Mr. Jack. Even Benny Pete hadn't said that to me.

I smiled.

It wasn't long before Bradford and I spent most of our waking time together, but that wasn't enough. We wanted to be together day and night. We decided we'd get our own apartment.

I was happy about that. He liked me and so I liked him. He was nice and genuinely seemed to care for me. He also liked my baby girl.

"I'll get a job," Bradford said. "We can get a one bedroom and take our time to furnish it."

So, he worked, and I enrolled in a technical school. I qualified for grant money, and with the money he made from working we were able to move into our apartment in no time.

Our apartment was small, but it was the first time I lived on my own in a place that I'd chosen and liked. I was happy, but I wanted my baby girl to live with me too. I was too scared to tell Mama. I was also scared at the thought of being a mom. I didn't want to mess it up. My baby girl deserved the best.

Was Mama the best?

She seemed to love my baby girl so much and gave her the love I wished she given to me.

As soon as I graduated from technical school, they placed me with a good company. I was making $7 an hour, and I had great benefits.

Mama hadn't been happy about Bradford or me moving out. However, I was grown now, and she couldn't stop me. I was free to make my own choices.

I realized if I didn't live with her, it wasn't so hard to take her criticisms, and I wouldn't have to endure the silent treatment, which hurt more than anything she ever said.

I was happy in our new apartment with my new man. When we weren't at work, we spent every waking hour together. One night we were in bed watching TV.

"I love this show," I said to Bradford. "Don't you?"

He didn't answer.

"Bradford, did you hear me?"

He still didn't answer.

I got up and turned on the bedroom light. He was just staring but not moving.

"Hello!" I was afraid. "Don't you hear me talking to you?"

Then, he started shaking, and his eyes rolled back in his head. I was so scared. I never saw anyone behave that way. We didn't have a phone (this was well before cell phones were so popular). So, I jumped up, threw on my robe, and ran out of the apartment to his mom's apartment. Thankfully, she lived in the same complex.

"Ms. Connie," I said out of breath. "Something's wrong with Bradford. He is shaking and won't say anything."

"Oh," she threw up her hands nonchalantly. "He probably aint been taking his medicine."

"What medicine?" I was frantic but noticed that she really wasn't that concerned.

"I'll call the ambulance for you," she said. "They'll take care of it."

I was confused and full of questions. I was scared for Bradford. He was back at the apartment alone. I ran back to the apartment and found him still shaking violently. I slipped on some clothes and waited for the ambulance. Finally, they arrived and transported him to the hospital.

It turns out that Bradford had a secret of his own.

He'd been hit by a car as a kid and spent a month in a coma. When he woke up, he'd had to learn how to speak and walk all over again. Now, he suffered from seizures if he didn't take his medication three times a day.

"Why didn't you tell me?" I asked when he woke up later that evening. "I was so scared."

"I'm sorry," he said, smiling. "I didn't want you to feel like you had to take care of me."

"Boy, aint you tired of going to the hospital so much?" Bradford's sister Brooke was a sergeant in the military and pretty much kept everyone in line. "Y'all need to go on and get married," she continued. "This boy needs some insurance so he can get his meds and take them regularly."

She looked at me, and I looked at Bradford.

And just like that, a few months later, in April of 1989, we were married.

Brooke furnished our apartment. She took me shopping and bought everything we needed from dishes to furniture, to food. I was so grateful.

Marrying Bradford seemed a small price to pay for what she'd done for us.

Anyway, I'd always wanted my own home. Now, I'd have a husband. Maybe I could even have another baby boy.

It didn't take long for me to understand that there is a difference between a house and a home.

Chapter Three

'Kerry Wilson'

After Bradford and I got married, I went to Mama and told her I wanted my baby.

"You don't know what you doin'," she said. "Yall over there playin' house. This baby needs to stay here."

She was right. I didn't know what I was doing. But I knew I wanted my baby with me.

"I have a job now. I'm married, and we have a place to live. I can do it."

I was surprised at how I was able to speak up to Mama. She relented and gave me the silent treatment for a time, but soon got over it because I needed her to baby sit my baby while I worked.

"Can you babysit for me?" I asked. "I can pay you."

Mama agreed.

I wanted another baby, and I was hoping it would be a boy. Maybe I would stop feeling so bad if I had another son.

It took nearly two years, but in July of 1991 – on my birthday, I had my third child. As the baby made his debut, a sudden burst of tears came at the doctor's declaration.

"Mrs. James, you have a son."

Bradford Jr. (BJ) was such a happy baby. He and his big sister Alisha got along so well.

Alisha was very protective of him, and I was happy about that.

Later that year, my job promoted me, and we moved to Arizona. I was good at my job, and the pay was great. The company even paid the moving expenses on the stipulation that I remain employed there for two years.

I was married. I had my baby girl and a new son. My job was great, and I was making more money than I'd ever made, but I was worried because Bradford wasn't working.

Mama only gave me my baby girl because I told her I could take care of her. Now I had two babies, and with Bradford not working, I was afraid Mama would find out how tight things were and take both of my children.

While we were in Arizona, I found out why Bradford smiled so much. He didn't just smoke marijuana from time to time, he was addicted. This was also why he didn't take his medicine consistently and why he couldn't hold a steady job.

I loved Bradford and wanted our family to stay together, so I thought moving to Arizona would give us more time to work things out. Plus, I didn't want Mama to see that Bradford wasn't working.

Mama always said, "You can't put perfume on top of shit. It'll still be shit."

We arrived in Arizona, and right away things went from bad to worse. Bradford didn't get a job, so he stayed home with BJ while I worked. When I saw how comfortable he was with that arrangement, I knew I'd better do something about that. I tried to help.

"Why don't you enroll in school," I suggested. "Maybe if you have a trade, you can find a job. A lot of schools have job placement too."

Bradford and I had started Devington Career college together. He had gotten his school money and then stopped going to classes. I kept going, and they'd found me the job I had.

"I don't know what I want to do," he said without interest.

"Well," I said. "You like to cook. Why don't you go to culinary school?"

Bradford was a good cook. I suppose he got that from his mom, Ms. Connie, who worked for the military in an NCO (Non-Commissioned Officers) Club. I figured if he was doing something he enjoyed, it would make it seem less like work since clearly, he had an aversion to working.

"Nah, I don't wanna cook for a living," he said while rolling up a joint.

"You've got to do something," I pushed. "I need you to help me with these bills. I'll pay for the baby to go to daycare while you find a school and get enrolled."

I was determined to do all that I could to help him succeed. Thoughts of divorce had begun to creep into my head, and that frightened me.

How would I raise two children alone?

I had no one to talk to and resentment began to set in. It got so bad, I hated to see him eat (which was a lot!) because I was reminded that he wasn't contributing!

That wasn't something I was proud of, and I felt guilty for feeling that way, but it was the truth. Bradford's unemployment and drug addiction became one more thing that I had to keep secret.

Finally, after my constant urging, Bradford enrolled in a security school. He would drop me off at work, Alisha at school, and BJ at our neighbor's house. Melvin and Marva ran a daycare in their home and agreed to give us a discount since Melvin and Bradford had become friends.

Every two weeks, when I got paid, I gave Bradford money to give to Melvin and Marva for keeping our baby. A few months went by, and I decided to ask Bradford about school since he hadn't said much. I got the shock of my life.

"Oh yea," he said calmly. "I forgot to tell you. I stopped going."

"What?" I asked, thinking I'd heard him wrong. "When?"

"A few months back." He said. "Them people didn't like me."

"A few months back!" I was livid. "So, I've been paying Melvin and Marva for daycare all this time? What have you been doing?"

"Me and Melvin been hanging out," he said, still calm, which for some reason further infuriated me.

Melvin smoked marijuana too, but at least he did have a job.

I was hurt. I felt used. I wanted to lash out, hit him and hurt him, but I was afraid he'd leave.

Bradford just sat there, smiling. I realized he was high so whatever I was saying to him wasn't making an impact. Then a thought occurred to me.

"So, where are you getting the money for your drugs?" I asked, not sure I wanted to know the answer.

"Melvin," he said.

"Melvin?" I repeated. "You've got to be kidding me."

Melba was a stay at home mom while Melvin worked nights. So, the money I was giving Bradford to give to Melba was essentially given to Melvin to buy drugs for the two of them.

I knew then that our marriage was over. I just didn't know how to disentangle myself from him. I didn't want to put him out. We were thousands of miles from Indiana. And I knew what it felt like to be put out. Memories of Mama taking Alisha and leaving me in Arkansas flashed in front of me.

I couldn't do that to him. I felt trapped.

I continued to go to work, but I stopped giving Bradford money for daycare and insisted he stay home with the baby. Then he started using cash I'd give him for bills to buy drugs, so I purchased money orders instead. There were times Bradford would 'forget' to mail the money orders and then he started 'losing' them. The threat of us being evicted or having the electricity disconnected didn't stop Bradford from buying and using drugs.

I was too afraid to demand he get a job. I was too afraid to leave him. And I was too ashamed to talk to anyone about what was going on in my home. So, I suffered in silence.

"Hey, Iris," Kerry said. "How are you?"

"Hi Kerry," I responded and managed a smile. "I'm ok. How are you?"

"I'm ok too," she said, "but I'm not sure I believe that you are judging by the look on your face."

Kerry's response took me by surprise. Not many people noticed me, and usually when I had on my mask, I could fool people.

Mama had taught me how to wear a mask.

"Fix yo darn face," Mama would say whenever I was looking a way she didn't like. Then she'd hit me if I wasn't quick enough.

Now that I was grown, I was good at hiding my emotions behind a mask of unfeeling. Or so I thought.

"It's ok," she encouraged. "You can talk to me. I'm here to listen."

Kerry and I were the only two people of color hired from the Indiana office. We talked from time to time about work and being homesick. Kerry was pleasant and always nicely dressed.

"You're right," I confessed. "I'm not doing so well. It's almost Christmas, and I can't see how I'll get through the holidays. I want my kids to have a good Christmas."

I was making good money, but since I was paying all the bills, there wasn't anything left over after I paid rent, the car payment, electricity, the phone, and groceries. My son was still in pampers and was drinking formula. I was feeding two children and two adults on one salary. I was in over my head.

"Don't you worry," Kerry said. "Jehovah will provide."

"Jehovah?" I said and looked at her with what must have been a confused expression.

"Yes," she said. "I'm a Jehovah's Witness."

"Really?" And that's all I could manage.

Over the years I'd learned that the "people who wore white" were called Jehovah's Witnesses. They attended Kingdom Hall and went around the neighborhoods "witnessing" to communities.

Memories of all the times Mama had made me hide from them came back to me like a flood, and I was instantly embarrassed. I never knew why we hid from them.

Kerry seemed like a very nice person, and now that I knew she was a Jehovah's Witness, I was even more confused.

"Kerry," I said tentatively. "I have a question."

"Sure," she said. "You can ask me anything."

"What does it mean to be a Jehovah's Witness?" I asked.

Kerry explained it to me. Basically, she believed that if you don't accept God into your life and live according to His Word, when you die you are just dead.

That didn't seem like a harsh punishment to me. My whole life, I'd always heard that if you didn't follow God, you'd pay with burning in Hell forever and ever. I shared my thoughts with Kerry, and she laughed.

"Yea," she continued to laugh. "But God is not a vengeful God. He is a loving God, and He doesn't want to hurt His children. He wants to love us, and He wants us to love Him back."

That explanation made me want to know more about God. Up until then, I had been afraid of God. He seemed mean and uncaring. I wondered, if God existed, why had my life turned out so badly? The things that were done to me as a kid made no sense.

Why did God allow those things to happen to me? Didn't He love me?

A few weeks later, Kerry showed up at work with a trunk full of presents for my kids.

"I can't accept this," I said feeling embarrassed. I didn't want to be a charity case. "Besides, I thought you don't celebrate Christmas."

"I don't," Kerry said. "And this isn't about Christmas. This is about helping a friend do what she can't do."

I hugged her and quickly wiped at the tears that threatened to fall.

I still didn't understand why Mama hid from the Jehovah's Witnesses.

That experience with Kerry opened my eyes to a few things:

One, family is not just about blood.

Two, you don't have to agree in order to be accepting.

I realized that the kindest thing I could do for my son's father was to break my contract at work and move back to Indiana.

Chapter Four

'Anton Davis'

I moved back to Indiana in 1992, broke things off with Bradford, and found myself without a place to stay in the process.

The expense of moving (I before my contract expired) and the divorce cost me more than I had. I didn't have enough to secure an apartment. I was near a breakdown. I was afraid Mama would take my kids, and I was right.

"Give me them kids," she said harshly. "Go on and get yourself together. You don't need to be dragging them kids all over the place."

I felt horrible. I had failed. The family I thought I had was only a short-lived illusion.

I put my furniture in storage, left my kids with Mama, and moved in with a coworker named Kelly in order to save money for an apartment.

Kelly was single with no children, and for all intents and purpose, I was too.

I attempted to push down my feelings of depression by forcing myself to be happy.

For the first time since I was fifteen, I didn't have any obligations. I had never been a normal teenager – wild and crazy. And although I was nearly 23 years old, I realized I'd never truly been free.

My life had never been my own, until now.

Kelly was a clubber and convinced me it was fun. I had never gone to a club, so I decided

I wanted to see what the fuss was about. We went to clubs, stayed up late talking, and did whatever we wanted to do or did nothing at all. We slept late on the weekends and stayed out all night partying. I wasn't a teenager, but I was living like one. And it felt good to be free.

I didn't allow myself to think about my kids, the baby I'd placed for adoption, or what Mama must have thought about my life now. It hurt too much. So, I focused on having fun instead.

I was doing just that when I met Anton.

Kelly and I were at a club *Ebony and Ivory*. I loved to dance and would frequently dance by myself if I had to. I quickly learned that most men thought if they bought you a drink or danced with you once, they had the right to sit at your table and claim you for the rest of the night.

I didn't want to be claimed.

"Damn, Iris," Kelly whined. "We just got here. Can't we at least get seats before you hit the dance floor?"

"Nope," I said and snapped my fingers and shook my hips to the music. "You already know if you sit down, some dude will be there, blocking the view of the dance floor, trying to buy some drinks, and holding you hostage for the rest of the night."

"Well, I still ain't figured out what's wrong with that?" Kelly wrinkled up her nose and put her hands on her ample hips.

I had actually slimmed down since my divorce. Who had time or money to eat?! I went from a size 22 to a size 14 in no time. And because I was so tall, most people were surprised I wore a 14. For the first time in my life, I felt like I looked good.

Toni Braxton was hot in the music world, and her new album, "Another Sad Love Song" kept me on the dance floor.

"Love should have brought you home last night," I shouted over the music and kept

dancing. "You go on and sit. I'll be over later."

I made my way to the middle of the dance floor, and that's where I stayed for the next seven or eight songs. By the time I made my way back to the table, my hair was drenched as well as my clothes. But I didn't care about that. I felt exhilarated! I sat down long enough to order a drink, pay for it, drink it, and head back to the dance floor. Kelly rolled her eyes. She didn't move much, which explained her size 26 frame. But she had a pretty face, long and naturally curly hair, a quick comeback for everything, and was a self-proclaimed freak! The men loved her. There were many nights I heard screaming coming from her bedroom, and it wasn't Kelly doing the screaming!

I wasn't ready for all that. I wanted to be loved.

Although Bradford had been a huge disappointment, I missed being married. Instead of being sad, I was out living life and enjoying my freedom.

Until Anton showed up.

Anton was tall, light-skinned, clean-shaven, and smooth-talking.

I had been on the dance floor most of the night, but I wasn't tired at all. My hair and my clothes looked like I'd been doused in water. I was shocked to feel someone pulling me into them by my waist.

"What the-," I said but stopped midsentence. The perpetrator was smiling and put his fingers up to my lips to silence me.

"Get your hands off my lips," I shouted. I'd downed several drinks, and the liquid courage was in full effect. "I don't know where your hands have been!"

He laughed and leaned into my ear.

"I know where they'd like to be," he said and put his tongue in my ear.

A chill went down my spine, and I tingled. I jumped back and broke free from his embrace. This man was bold.

"Excuse you," I said. "I don't know you like that!"

"But baby, you can," he said and began dancing with me.

The brother had moves, and soon people were stopping to watch us. I wasn't Iris when I drank, which is why I had begun to drink more than I should. Alcohol allowed me to be free. I could say and do whatever I wanted.

"What's your name?"

"Iris," I said. "And you?"

"Anton," he said and smiled at me like he knew something I didn't.

"So, Iris," Anton pulled me closer to him. "Where is this going to end?"

Toni was talking about how someone was making her temperature rise. I understood it perfectly. Anton's effect on me was making me nervous. I knew I had to get away from him before I did something I'd regret.

"With me leaving," I said and walked off the dance floor. Thankfully, Kelly had given me the signal that it was time to go.

We walked out of the club, and I got in on the passenger side of her car. Kelly always drove because she didn't drink. She was a tiger on her own.

Just as I closed the door, Anton came up to the car and knocked on the window.

"Get rid of him for me, Kelly," I knew she could and would.

She reached across me and rolled down my window.

"WHAT?"

Anton backed up with his arms in the air like Kelly was the police. "Damn, baby, I was just trying to tell you ladies to drive safe. I got what I came for." He said curiously and walked away.

"That was easy," I said. Kelly and I laughed.

But the joke was on me.

The next day there was a loud banging on the apartment door. I knew Kelly wasn't budging, so I jumped up prepared to give whoever it was a mean mug.

I yanked open the door, and there was Anton. He looked just as good in the daylight as he had last night under the club lights.

"What are you-," I said, but before I could get the rest of my sentence out, he held up my purse.

"I think this is yours." He said with a wide grin.

"How did you get my purse?" I asked, trying to remember where I'd left it.

"You left it on the table in the club," he said, still smiling.

I didn't remember that but didn't want him to know. I took it and quickly looked inside. My lipstick, driver's license, and keys were there, but my money wasn't. I knew I'd had at least $40.

"You took my money?" I asked.

"Money," he said. "I didn't see no money, lil mama. I just looked at the driver's license, so I could return it to you."

I wasn't going to argue with him. Maybe I'd left it in the club. I did remember buying a few drinks.

"Well, thanks," I said and waited for him to walk off. But he didn't.

"Hey, since I returned your purse, the least you can do is go to breakfast with me."

I stood there and thought about it. No one had ever tried so hard to get my attention. I was flattered.

"Now?" I asked.

"Why not?" He pushed.

I didn't have a good answer, and I was hungry. So, I agreed.

"OK," I said. "Let me take a shower, and I'll meet you at Denny's on Post Road."

"Let me in, and I'll wait for you," he said, walking towards me.

"Um no," I said, putting my hand out to keep him in place. "I don't know you like that."

"You can if you cooperate," he laughed.

"You're moving way too fast for me," I said, suddenly feeling uneasy. "Maybe this isn't a good idea."

"Look," he said, becoming serious. "If I was a criminal, would I have given you back your purse?"

I guessed he had a point, but I still wasn't going to let him in.

"You can meet me at Denny's, or you can just go back to where you been," I said confidently. I wondered if I was still under the influence.

"Ok. Ok. Ok," he said, giving up. "I'll meet you there."

Within months, Anton and I were an item. He was always at the apartment. Kelly was mad because she said he was there too much.

"Why don't you go over to his place sometime?" She grumbled. "It's like having a third roommate."

Anton *was* there a lot, but he lived with his sister and slept on her couch. He said she had a boyfriend and wanted her privacy, so it was just easier if he stayed there with me. Besides, I liked having him there. It was nice coming home to someone who wanted me.

Since Anton got off work before me, I gave him my key so he wouldn't have to wait for me to get home. Kelly didn't like it, but I didn't care.

One day I got home and didn't see Anton's car. Kelly worked second shift, so I decided to sit in the parking lot and wait. An hour went by, and Anton still hadn't come home, so I drove to the gas station and called him, but he didn't answer.

I drove back to the parking lot and still didn't see his car. I waited several hours and finally decided to go upstairs and wait for him by the door. For some reason, I tried the knob and discovered the door was unlocked.

I opened it and walked inside.

When I got to my bedroom, I opened the door and noticed an emptiness. The room had been a bit crowded with all of Anton's things, but now, as I looked around, I realized his things were gone. I opened his dresser drawers and the closet, and sure enough, all of his clothes were gone.

I looked on the dresser and realized there was a note:

Iris, I am so sorry. But I can't do this anymore. Please don't hate me, Anton.

Under the note was the apartment key.

I was numb.

What had I done? Where was he? Why did he do this?

I had so many questions, but no answers.

I sat on the bed and found myself staring. There it was, the white wall.

Were all walls white or just the ones in my life?

I took a shower and got into bed. I wanted to cry but couldn't. This was my own fault. I should never have trusted him.

My thoughts went back to the first time I met him.

Had he stolen my money from my purse? Had Mama been right about me?

Was I ignorant?

In spite of how he left, I kept thinking he'd come back. Toni's song, "Seven Whole Days" became the gauge by which I determined how long I'd wait. Day seven came and went, and there was still no word or sign of Anton.

"Where's old dude," Kelly asked, and it almost seemed she had a smirk on her face.

"I broke it off," I lied. I'd never admitted to being dumped in such an awful way. Better to keep that secret to myself.

I threw away whatever I had that reminded me of Anton, refused to cry, and was determined to move on with my life.

Anton was just a reminder that I wasn't worth the effort when it came to men.

The single life wasn't for me. After a while, dancing and drinking failed to keep me from what I was feeling. I was lonely and missed my kids.

I focused more on saving and soon I was able to afford an apartment. I found an apartment, and moved in. I got my kids back, and Mama continued to babysit for me. This time in addition to paying her for keeping them, I agreed to buy our dinner from her each evening too.

It saved me from having to cook each night, so I didn't mind.

Weeks after I moved into my own place, I walked into the grocery store, and there was Anton. He was with a woman, and the woman was holding a baby that looked just like Anton! Anton's eyes met mine, and I turned around and walked out of the store. It felt like I had been stabbed.

I was humiliated. I was hurt. I was confused.

What was it about me?

I was beginning to see a pattern. The men in my life never hung around very long.

Why did everyone leave me?

Why wasn't I good enough?

Even Mr. Jack had left.

Chapter Five

'William White'

I was familiar with Masons. My brothers were very active. So, when I met William White, who was a mason and friends with my brothers, I figured I could trust him.

After my fiasco with Anton, I desperately wanted to trust and love someone again.

"Guess who wants your phone number," my sister, Lola, asked. She and her girls had moved to Indiana a few years after I did.

"Who," I wondered.

"William White." And then she laughed.

"William?" I said and laughed with her, although I wasn't sure what we were laughing about.

"Yea, he wanted to know if I thought you'd be interested in him."

"Isn't he with Cassandra?" I asked.

"Nah, that relationship isn't working. He is about to move back to Arkansas."

Moving back to Arkansas had been on my mind for some time. I'd decided that city life just wasn't for me. Although most of my family lived in Indiana, the cold, dark winters made me sad.

So, knowing that William was moving wasn't a deterrent for me. I actually thought, *maybe this is some sort of sign*.

Lola gave William my number, and he and I talked on the phone. When he moved to Arkansas, we continued corresponding via letters. No one had written me letters since Benny Pete, my high school sweetheart. It felt good. I read them carefully over and over. Each time, I was left feeling loved and cared for.

William was shorter than the other guys I'd been in relationships with. He was dark-skinned, he wore glasses, and he smoked cigarettes. He also drank. Lola told me that he had a "pee bag" too.

"What's a 'pee bag'?" I asked Lola.

"It's a bag that is connected to him that he pees in," Lola explained.

That didn't make sense to me, but I decided I didn't care. I had been born with a disability, too, so if William was able to overlook my faults, I could certainly overlook his.

"I want you to come to Arkansas and meet my family," William announced.

"Really?" I said flattered. It meant something when a man wanted you to meet his family. I felt like I was important to him.

I flew to Little Rock, and William picked me up from the airport. We dropped off my luggage at his mom's house where he was living.

"I'll be getting a job and my own place real soon," he said. "I need my space."

I understood. When I moved from Indiana to Arizona, it had been challenging trying to figure out everything.

William and his mom lived in a trailer. I was surprised, not impressed, but determined not to show it on my face. I knew better than to judge a book by its cover.

We walked inside, and my heart sank.

This book was exactly what it looked like on the outside.

The trailer was hot, cramped, and there were roaches. It seemed like Mrs. White hadn't changed furniture since the 70s. But I was grateful she was allowing me to stay there during my visit.

"Mama," William began, "This is Iris. She's the younger sister of several of my lodge brothers back in Indiana."

"Hey," Mrs. White said. "Welcome back to Arkansas. You look real pretty in your romper."

I smiled and thanked her for the compliment. Since Anton, I'd dropped quite a bit of weight. That was the only good thing about a breakup; I usually lost a lot of weight. I was now a size 10, and with my height, I looked really slim. The romper I was wearing was flattering, and I actually felt pretty.

Mrs. White didn't look like William. She was light-skinned, had long fine hair, and was in good shape for a woman her age.

She spit, and I realized she dipped snuff. I immediately thought about Aunt Ethelene, Mama's half-sister in Holly Grove, who dipped snuff. I hoped Mrs. White wasn't the kissing kind like Aunt Ethelene had been. She hugged me instead, and I was relieved.

"I'm cooking," she announced. "Food should be ready in a little while."

"Mama, I told you I was taking Iris to Cajuns," William said roughly. "You don't listen!"

I was shocked to hear him speaking to his mama like that! I stepped back expecting her to hit him, but instead, she yelled back at him.

"Well, Bill," she began and looked at me with a look I couldn't decipher. "I had to cook anyway so y'all may as well stay here and eat with me."

"I'm not staying here," he continued to shout. "You can eat by yourself!"

He stormed out of the trailer and back to the car. I stood there awkwardly not knowing what to do or say. I was embarrassed and confused.

Why was he so angry?

I thought it was nice that she wanted to cook and have us all eat together.

Finally, William came back in with my luggage, pushed past us, and disappeared down the hallway. When he came back, he sat down like nothing had happened. So, I sat down on the sofa next to him. Mrs. White sat down, too, and grabbed the house phone. She dialed the numbers and began talking.

"Bill acting crazy again," she said into the phone. "All I was trying to do was be nice."

Suddenly William stood up, walked over to his mother, and snatched the phone from her.

She stood up and said, "Bill, you don't have to act like that."

"Mama, I don't need you starting stuff," he was shouting now, and the anger in his eyes was like fire. "You can't control what I do. I'm a grown man."

"I ain't trying to control you. I'm just trying to be nice. Y'all don't have to be here."

That was the wrong thing to say. William slammed the receiver back on the phone and flung it at the wall. I jumped, Mrs. White burst into tears, and stormed out of the room.

I didn't know what was going on or why things had gotten heated so quickly. Then, I heard sniffles. William was crying!

"What's the matter," I asked full of worry and concern.

"I know you're going to leave me now for sure," he said while huge tears fell down his cheeks.

"No I'm not," I reassured him. "I understand."

But I didn't. All I knew is that I'd never seen a man cry before. He must have really been in love with me to worry so much about what I thought. I sat down next to him and hugged him, hoping he knew that I would be there for him.

We went to Cajuns, had some drinks, ate, and even danced. By the time we got back to the trailer, Mrs. White was already in bed asleep.

"I hope you don't mind sleeping in my room," William said. "I wanted us to be together. I won't bother you."

I was flattered again. He and I hadn't been intimate. We talked about it in our letters, but the opportunity had never come up until now. He pulled me into an embrace, and we kissed. I felt something wet on my stomach, so I looked down. The whole side of my shirt was wet. William looked down too and started cussing.

"Damn," he said in exasperation. "This always happens. I'm so sorry, Iris."

He rushed out of the room, and I stood there confused. The smell of urine was strong. In the small, hot trailer, the smell became nauseating, but I didn't want William to know how I felt, so I forced myself not to think about it.

When William came back into the room, I had gotten my nightgown and toiletry bag out of my luggage.

"Where's the bathroom?" I asked. "I want to shower and change."

"Did I get much on you?" William asked clearly embarrassed. "I'm so sorry."

"It's ok," I said. "I know you can't help it." I was sympathetic. Having my own handicap made me sensitive to things that people couldn't control.

"Are you grossed out" He asked.

"No," I said. And realized I wasn't really, but it was uncomfortable.

I went to the bathroom and cleaned up. When I came back, William was already in bed. Over the course of the night, more urine spilled onto the bed and me. I tried to get up to clean myself, but he insisted that he wanted to hold me. So, I laid there, wet. William wrapped me in his arms tightly, and I laid awake most of the night. I finally fell asleep from exhaustion.

And that was how things went for the duration of our relationship. I hid my feelings, and he poured his onto me. He was offensive, inconsiderate, and at times downright mean.

They say the way a man treats his mama is how he will treat you. In William's case, that was true. The verbal abuse was one thing, but the mental abuse was even worse. It was like living with Mama all over again but ten times worse. The more he drank, the more abusive he became.

And still, I married him. In 1995, he asked me, and I didn't have the heart to say no. We were already living together anyway.

My kids needed a home and a father. So, I put my feelings aside, thinking I was doing what was best for them.

I wanted Mama to see that I could provide a good home for my children. I wanted her to be proud of me for something good.

But it seemed the harder I tried to please others, the more misery I created for myself.

One year, William's birthday rolled around, and I decided I'd buy him a 50-disc CD changer stereo. I knew how much he loved music, and I wanted to surprise him. The store delivered the system, and the kids and I waited for him to come home.

William didn't come home after work.

The kid's bedtime came, and I put them to bed and told them I'd wake them when he got home.

Around midnight, William still wasn't home, and I was worried. I called him, but he didn't answer. I even called his mother, but she said she didn't know where he was either.

The next morning as I was dressing the kids for school and daycare, William finally called.

"How could you do this to me?" He yelled into the phone.

"Do what?" I asked completely confused.

"You know what you've been doing," he said. "I don't have to explain it."

This was Dr. Buckhead all over again. Someone telling me that I'd done something, but I didn't have any clue or memory of what it was! It was completely frustrating and unnerving.

"I can't do this with you anymore," he continued. "I want a divorce."

It wasn't the first time William had threatened me with divorce. That word had been hurled at me more times than I could count, and I was tired of the threats.

Whatever William wanted from me, clearly, I wasn't able to give it to him.

I was tired of hanging on to someone who didn't want me. In defeat, I let go.

"Ok," I agreed.

"What?" William yelled into the phone. "What did you say?"

"I said ok," I cried. "We can do the divorce."

William wasted no time leaving and didn't look back. I never saw him again. And I had to move.

There was no time to cry over him or the end of another marriage. I had two children and no place to live.

I didn't have any money, so I had to sell all of my furniture to get the deposit and rent money for my new apartment. I moved my clothes and other belongings into trash bags with my car.

It was humiliating and so sad. But I didn't want my children to see my pain. So, I pushed it down.

At night, when things were quiet, I allowed the questions to overtake me.

What was it about me that left me unable to hold the love or attention of a man? What was I missing? Would I ever find lasting love?

Mama had always said I was an ignorant ass fool, and it turned out she was right.

Iris M. Williams

I believed William would be there always, yet once again, I was starting over.

Chapter Six

'Gregg Harrison'

William quickly filed for a divorce in 1999. I found out I had been wife number seven.

After I moved, I got a second job and somehow managed to keep my head above water. Summer came, and I sent the kids to Indiana to stay with Mama for the summer.

Since I was home alone on the weekends and needed something to do to get over my heartbreak, I agreed to go to Memphis with Benny Pete's sisters from Holly Grove. We'd all been childhood friends, and it was fun seeing them and catching up.

"Eyeball," Rita Pane shouted. "Guhl, where the hell you been so long?" I grinned at the nickname. Rita said I had big eyes.

Rita was Benny Pete's younger sister. The Panes were big on nicknames. The whole family had one: Benny Pete was called Joe Man. Rita was called Peter Tail and Eileen was called Tabby Cat.

Rita was stout, compact, and no nonsense. She always wore Levi's, Nike's and NEVER carried a purse. Rita was wearing her hair short and natural before it was popular.

"Just living," I said quietly. I didn't want to get into what all I'd been doing. I was ashamed to say having babies and getting married. By this time, I'd had three children by three different men and been married and divorced twice. It wasn't something I wanted to discuss. "What have you been doing?"

"Shit, just working." Rita and her family were known for cussing. Their parents had cursed too. Even the little children had cussed. Mama wouldn't allow me to cuss, but she hadn't seemed to mind that the Panes had done so.

I was looking forward to our trip to Memphis. I'd heard that Beale Street was great for a good time!

I drove from Little Rock to Holly Grove, and then we all piled into Rita Pane's truck. We were headed for what I hoped would be a weekend of fun.

"Peter Tail, you need to slow yo ass down," her sister Eileen yelled from the back seat as she popped the top on a Budweiser.

I felt the same way, but I didn't want to say anything. However, Eileen wasn't concerned about our safety.

"You gonna make me waste my damn beer," she continued and offered a few cuss words for emphasis.

A dog crossed the road and Rita swerved, but in the direction of the dog.

"Rita," I yelled. "Don't you see that dog?"

"Yea," Rita shouted back. "I hate a dog. I'll run in a ditch to kill a dog. They need to stay they ass out the road."

I closed my eyes and laid my head back against the headrest. My life was in such shambles; I honestly wasn't concerned about dying. It was living that worried me.

In spite of Rita breaking all the traffic rules, we arrived safely in Memphis, checked into our hotel, and decided to go to Beale Street to get dinner. It was still early, so we figured we'd eat first, go back to the room, shower and change, and go back on Beale Street to listen to some music and to have some drinks.

B.B. King was the restaurant we chose. It was loud and full of a mixed crowd. The food was great. We couldn't talk over the music, so we ate and left as soon as we finished.

Back in the room, Eileen decided we needed to set some ground rules.

"If anyone thinking about getting' they groove on, make sure you wear a damn condom and put the privacy sign on the door," she burped loudly. "I don't wanna see y'all ass up in the air."

We all laughed. Eileen was always saying something crude, and she always had a beer can in her hand.

There was a part of me hoping I'd find romance, but another part of me knew romance wasn't what it would be if I did found someone here. However, I held out hope as I dressed. We had decided to dress alike in black Levi's, leopard print shirts, and black flats. We wanted to be comfortable since we'd be doing a bunch of walking.

It takes three women with one bathroom three times as long to get dressed, so by the time we left the room, it was well after 10! As we stepped off the elevator, we heard music coming from the lobby.

"What in hell is going on over there," Rita asked and walked over to see.

We followed her and discovered the hotel had a club in the lobby! The man at the door said that hotel guests got in free, so we showed our room keys and walked inside.

The atmosphere was electrifying. We walked around, found a table, and sat down. When the waitress came over to take our drink orders, we'd already decided we wouldn't go to Beale Street that night. There was too much going on in here!

We drank our drinks, danced a bit, and talked and laughed. We were having a great time. Then, something caught Rita's eyes, and she hollered.

"Damn!" She said and pointed towards the door.

We all looked and saw a group of well-dressed men in suits entering the club.

As if summoned, several of them came directly to our table and began making small talk with us. I didn't say much. Although I had drunk several drinks, liquid courage wasn't working for me that night.

I was asked to dance, and I accepted several invitations. Then, I decided to go to the restroom to see what I was looking like. As I stepped into the hotel lobby, one of the guys from the group approached me.

"Hey," he said and flashed a confident smile at me. "You ok?"

"Yea," I said and smiled back. "I'm ok, just taking a bathroom break."

I kept walking and did what I had to do. When I stepped back into the lobby, I was surprised to see him still standing in the same spot talking on his cell phone. As I passed him, he quickly ended the call.

"Excuse me," he said and matched his stride with mine. "Do you have a minute?"

I stopped and waited for him to catch up to me.

"Sure," I said and suddenly felt nervous.

What could he possibly want with me, I wondered.

"The guys and I are shutting down for the night. We have some drinks we didn't even open. I was wondering if you wanted to get something for you and your girls."

"That would be great," I said. I looked towards the door of the club but didn't see any of my friends. Then, I looked back at him and decided he was safe enough. I followed him to the elevators.

He made small talk, and I learned they were fraternity brothers. They were hosting their annual conference in the hotel. They had a large suite on the top floor. As we stepped off the elevators, he pulled me into his arms and put his lips to my ear.

"I've had my eye on you all night. There's something different about you." He whispered. "Think I can find out what it is?"

I allowed him to continue to embrace me. Then, he led me into his suite. He had magnetism and charisma. I'd never had a guy like this approach me. I was flattered, intrigued, and definitely turned on. I think the liquid courage had crept up on me.

The room was surrounded by large floor to ceiling windows, and the Memphis skyline was gorgeous. He turned on some music, and we slow danced. Then, he kissed me, and I melted in his arms. I'd never been treated in such a gentle manner before. It felt great.

Afterward, we laid in each other's arms on the sofa. Neither of us spoke. Suddenly, there was hard knocking on the door.

"Eyeball," Rita yelled. "Are you in there? Are you ok?" She started cussing then. I could tell she had been worried.

"I'm fine," I yelled back. "I'll be down shortly."

He and I laughed and realized it was time to rejoin the group.

Later that night, while the girls slept, all I heard were Eileen's snores and my frantic voice:

I didn't even get his name!

I'd had a one-night stand.

But instead of feeling ashamed, I actually felt pretty good. This one-time encounter with a stranger had felt more intimate than any relationship I'd had.

How was that possible?

The next day, the girls drilled me as I expected.

"Eyeball," Rita said as we sat down to breakfast. She cussed me out again for disappearing. "And who was that guy? What happened? And why didn't you tell us you were leaving? We thought something bad had happened!"

I had lain awake part of the night trying to decide how I'd answer all the questions I knew the girls would have for me. Since I couldn't think of any that would be believable, I kept my answers vague, and let them think I knew more than I wanted to tell them.

"I'm sorry," I began. "Things just kind of happened, and I didn't have time to let y'all know. It was cool. We chilled."

Eileen looked at me sideways. Rita and I were drinking coffee and juice, but she had brought a Budweiser with her from the room. When the waitress came over to take our order, Eileen glared at her and dared her to say something about it. The waitress chose not to make a fuss.

Thankfully, the girls didn't pressure me for details, so we quickly continued with our day.

First, we shopped; then, we had lunch. By the time we got back to the room, we were all ready for a nap. We still had another night in Memphis and decided we needed to get some sleep if we were going to make it to Beale Street.

We slept longer than we intended, and by the time we woke up, showered, and dressed, it was well past 10 again. As we entered the hotel lobby, we saw the same group of guys standing outside the club entrance.

The mystery man and I locked eyes and smiled. I was embarrassed. I never expected to see him again. The realization of what we'd done the night before hit me hard, and without the liquid courage, I contemplated going back to the room to hide.

I'd enjoyed every minute of our encounter, but I didn't know what he thought of me.

What kind of woman has a one-night stand?

"Hey," he said again. "Can we go somewhere and talk for a minute?"

I waved at the girls and told them I'd meet up with them later.

"I realized this morning that I didn't get your name last night," he said and smiled at me.

"I know," I said and laughed with him. "I realized the same thing. It's Iris."

"Wow, that's beautiful," he said. "I've never known an Iris before. My name is Gregg."

Gregg and I talked for hours.

I found out that Gregg was married. I wasn't upset about it because it hadn't been like he was trying to pull the wool over my eyes. We'd just been two people in need of companionship. Gregg told me his marriage was in trouble.

"No matter what I do or say, I can't seem to get through to her," he said sadly. "I cook, clean, help with the children, provide a nice living, and even run her bath water and light candles. She just doesn't seem interested in me anymore."

I couldn't imagine why anyone wouldn't want him or respond to him. Gregg was average height and build. He was an engineer, educated, articulate, and very handsome. From what I could see, he was definitely a catch. Then again, he was here with me, so maybe the problem in his marriage was that he wasn't home enough.

He was here with me now, and I was happy about that. I enjoyed our conversation. Not since Benny Pete had a man talked so openly and freely with me about his life and feelings.

Gregg did most of the talking, and I listened.

I was too embarrassed to tell him about my life. I told him the basics, just enough so that he wouldn't notice that I wasn't talking. I got the sense that he needed to talk anyway, so I let him.

The girls came to check on me again and found me standing in the hallway outside of our room talking. I'd missed the entire night of partying. They went inside the room, and I knew they were probably disappointed that I hadn't joined them in the club.

I left Memphis with Gregg's phone number and the promise to keep in touch. And we did.

He and I met pretty regularly, and it was great. We talked a lot, and he became a friend.

Turns out the reason Gregg's wife hadn't responded to him is because there was someone else. She wanted a divorce, and he agreed.

His divorce changed things for me. Now that he was single, I knew it was just a matter of time before he broke my heart.

As long as he was married, I hadn't had to worry over anything 'real' until now. Now, there was an elephant in the room.

I didn't want to develop expectations.

Why would he choose me, anyway?

Gregg was smart, an engineer, and had class.

I was an ignorant ass fool. Mama's words had been proven over and over again. My life was evidence that she'd been right all along.

What could I possibly offer a man like that?

I couldn't shake Mama's words from my brain, and slowly I began to distance myself from Gregg, knowing that I wasn't good enough.

He kept asking me what was wrong, but eventually, he moved on just as I knew he would.

However, since it'd been my idea, I didn't have to cry about it.

Although he didn't pursue me romantically, over the years, Gregg and I stayed in touch.

We often laughed about our "almost one-night stand."

I wonder what could have been if I could have gotten Mama out of my head.

Chapter Seven

'Donald Ingram'

My relationships and subsequent marriages to Bradford James and William White had both lasted around five years each.

Was five years the shelf life of a marriage?

After my divorce from William, I felt like all the air had been let out of my life. I was wary of love and didn't want any part of it. That was another reason I didn't pursue anything with Gregg; I just wasn't sure I could trust love again.

I lost my second job. Living on my own and taking care of my kids became hard and stressful. There never seemed to be enough of anything, and most days, I just wanted to stay in bed and cover my head.

Still, I had to press on. All my kids had was me.

I frequently had to decide between what was necessary and what was optional. There were things I knew I had to take care of because if I didn't, things could be worse. For instance, maintenance on my car was essential, so I could get to the places where I needed to go. Therefore, I made sure to get oil changes regularly.

As I pulled into the lube shop, the technician directed me to come forward. When I stepped out of the car, he took my information and kept staring at me.

"Would you like a Coke?" He asked politely as I exited the car.

"No," I said, "But I would like a Sprite instead."

I drank Coke, but I was tired of taking whatever people offered me. I wanted to assert myself, even if it was in a small way.

He brought me the Sprite as I sat waiting in the cool customer waiting room. I thanked him and sat down. I could see him working on my car, and from time to time, he'd glance up and smile at me. I smiled back and returned to reading my magazine.

What should have only taken 30-45 minutes ended up taking more than 3 hours!

"We stripped a screw," Shawn, the manager, said to me. "We're ordering a tool that can get it off, and as soon as my guy gets back from the parts store, we'll have it off in no time."

"Ok," I said with a sigh. It was the weekend, but I didn't have anything to do, so I continued to wait patiently.

Eventually, I was on my way. Shawn had given me a handful of carwash coupons and apologized profusely for the mix-up.

Over the next few weeks, I went to the carwash at least once a week, and each time, I saw the guy who'd worked on my car. He smiled but never made a move.

He was handsome and strong, and I noticed he wasn't wearing a wedding ring. One Saturday, as I pulled out of the carwash, Shawn, the manager, was there. I let down my window and motioned for him to come to my car.

"Hey Shawn," I said. "I have a question."

"Sure, what's up?"

"Is that guy married?" I asked boldly. Maybe I needed to take my love life into my own hands.

Shawn looked where I was pointing and shook his head. "Donald?" He said and smiled. "Nah, he's not married."

With boldness I didn't know I had, I said, "Can you give him my number?"

I scribbled my number on a piece of paper and handed it to Shawn. As I drove off, my nerves got the best of me, and I questioned my judgment.

Why did I do that? What would make him call me? If he were interested, he'd have asked ME for my number!

A few days went by without a call from Donald, so I figured he wasn't interested. Then, one day I was in the laundromat, and my phone rang. It was a number I didn't' recognize.

"Hello," I said.

"Hey," he said. "This is Donald. Shawn gave me your number."

"Oh hi," I said suddenly embarrassed and at a loss for words. "How are you?"

"I'm ok," he said. "What are you doing?"

"I'm at the laundromat," I responded. "The one on Geyer Springs by the Subway."

"I know where that is," he said. "Can I stop by to see you? I'm headed out of town but want to see you before I go."

"Yea," I said realizing I was looking crazy. It was laundry day, and I hadn't bothered to do more than put on shorts and a t-shirt.

Donald showed up and was wearing starched jeans and a button-up collar shirt. He looked really nice.

"I've never seen you out of your uniform," I said. "You look nice."

"Thanks," he laughed. "So, do you."

I didn't think so, but I was glad he said it anyway. We made small talk; then, he announced that he had to leave.

"I'll be back on Sunday," he said. "But when I get back, I'll call you. Maybe we can go to the movies."

"I'd like that," I said with a huge grin.

Don and I dated a short time, and before long, he had moved in with me. It was my suggestion. He was at my place every night anyway. The kids loved him, and things were just going well. He helped me with my bills, fixed things, and was very caring of my needs. I had never had anyone do so much for me, and I was very grateful.

Is gratitude enough to build a life around?

One night, I put the kids to bed early, lit some candles, and bought a bottle of wine. Don was on the balcony, smoking. I wished he didn't smoke, but I figured it was a small flaw that I could overlook.

He came in and seemed surprised.

"What's all this?" He asked.

"Just thought I'd do something nice," I said. "Do you like it?"

"I do," he said and noticed the glass of wine.

"Would you like some wine?" I asked. "I wasn't sure if you preferred red or white."

"Yes," he said looking strange. "Any kind is fine."

We drank the wine, and he decided he'd go get another one. When he returned, he had two bottles, and we drank those too. We both loosened up, laughed, and enjoyed ourselves.

It became a nightly thing.

Don would show up for dinner and bring two bottles of wine. I just thought he was generous, but it turned out Don was an alcoholic.

Years later, he blamed me for his relapse. He said he'd been trying to quit drinking when he met me, and my invitation to drink wine had derailed his efforts.

Don's past was just as painful as mine. He had issues with his mom, too, but wouldn't acknowledge the fully. I only knew what I knew because he wasn't engaged with her like I wasn't engaged with my mom.

Don had been raised by his grandparents and had very old-fashioned values.

"All a man is supposed to do is provide," Don had told me when I'd complained about his lack of communication, help with the children, or housework.

Don didn't have any children, and I was happy about that because it meant I didn't have to deal with any "baby mamas."

My kids loved him, mostly because he didn't discipline them and gave them whatever they wanted. I think it was his way of making sure they loved him.

I was happy that they were happy, so I overlooked a lot of things.

I didn't like it that Don played my children against me. If I told them no, he'd go against what I said and give it to them. I told him that wasn't the way to raise kids, but he said it didn't hurt for them to have things.

In spite of obvious red flags, I married Donald in June of 2000. He was involved to the extent he wanted to be when things were going well, but when the kids acted up, he was quick to remind me that those were "my damn kids."

Even though he was an alcoholic, Don worked hard, and while the financial security was good, not having him present in the relationship made me feel like a single woman.

He couldn't understand what I meant by him not being there and would always say, "Woman, I'm here. What more do you want?"

I knew I shouldn't have married him, but I did. His mama didn't want us to let the wedding decorations she'd made for his sister's wedding the year before, go to waste.

I'd gotten married for similar reasons (to help someone else), and so this one seemed as good as any of those.

Don wasn't physically or verbally abusive. His abuse was subtle. Most of the time I was convinced that I was losing my mind.

If I didn't do what he wanted or did something he didn't want, he'd ignore me.

The silent treatment was a tactic that Mama used frequently.

Because it worked.

I knew that if I did what Donald wanted, life would be so much easier.

He even told me that having sex with him once a week on Wednesdays was all that was needed for us to have a pleasant week.

So, what was one night in exchange for a week of peace?

I made sure to do whatever he wanted because it made my life much easier. He was much more pleasant when he was getting his way.

However, because Don drank every night (he'd graduated from wine to whisky quickly), if he was unhappy, he'd let me know and not in a nice way.

Soon, I realized that if he drank more than two cups of alcohol, I was in trouble. So, I watched him, and when he made his third drink, I announced my retirement to bed.

Living with an alcoholic was a nightmare. I felt trapped, smothered, and defeated. But this was marriage number three.

If this didn't work, who'd want to marry a woman with three failed marriages?

I wanted to be married, but I also wanted to be happy and loved.

While my home life was in turmoil, my professional life seemed to be on track. I'd just landed a new job and was being paid very well. With Don's income and mine combined, we were able to live a life free of financial worry.

We bought a large home in Maumelle, I upgraded to a Cadillac, and 3-4 times a year, we took great vacations. Our bank accounts were large, and our credit was nearly perfect.

By society's standards, I had made it.

So, why didn't I feel good? Why was there this nagging emptiness that haunted me day and night? Why was I so restless?

I tried filling the void with shopping, but no matter how many coach purses, shoes, clothes, or expensive jewelry I acquired, nothing brought me joy. The more things I collected, the worse my personal life became until I couldn't take it anymore.

I could no longer hold it all in. I began talking back to Don and rebelling in small ways. Where once I'd ask him if it was ok to go someplace, now I began telling him where I was going.

My change created turmoil for him; he began drinking more and having nasty outbursts. Sometimes, they happened in front of others.

It was Barack Obama's inauguration night, and we decided to have a party to celebrate. My friends were over, and so were Don's friends. We had plenty of food and drinks. At the end of the night, when it was just Don, my girlfriends, and me, the truth came out.

"My wife gonna be mad at me in the morning," Don said slurring his words. "But I'm going to say it anyway. She not in my heart." He said and shook his head back and forth violently as if to emphasize that he meant it.

The room was silent, and Rita spoke first.

"Don," she said and laughed. "You don't mean that. You're just drunk."

I knew Rita was trying to soften the blow, but she couldn't. I was hurt and embarrassed but also enlightened. Suddenly, everything made sense. This was why he did and said the things he did and said.

He wasn't in love with me.

From that moment on, I stopped trying. I knew the danger of that decision. I'd never had a relationship that I didn't carry. If I didn't do the work that was needed to keep us together, the relationship always fell apart.

Still, I didn't want to let go. I liked the life I had and didn't want to give up all that I'd accumulated. On the surface, we had a good life. Well, that's the picture we painted. Even the girls were convinced that Don's outburst was just because he was drunk, but I knew better.

For a time, I continued to pretend until I couldn't anymore.

I prayed and asked God to help me do what I didn't have the strength to do.

Three times Donald asked me for a divorce, and finally, I agreed.

I don't think he meant it, though. I think it was just a scare tactic. I think it was a way to control me, and in the past, it had worked.

"You're hurting me," he said one night before I left. "Don't do this."

My things were packed, and my mind was made up. The movers were coming, and I had already moved into the spare bedroom. Too much had been said, and too much had been done.

I was tired of hiding my tears under the shower and laying under a man once a week who confessed he didn't love me.

What was the point of staying?

Then, he cried, and just like with William, my heart broke for him. I wondered if I was making the right decision. I pondered if I should stay.

The next day brought clarity.

Don was drinking, and we were watching television. A commercial aired, and it spoke of emotional abuse.

"What is that?" I asked, confused. I knew what verbal and physical abuse was, but emotional abuse was a new term.

"Ha, ha," Don laughed. "That's what I do to you."

I looked at him and shook my head as if to lift a fog.

Had he really said that?

He went about his business as per usual, but my world stopped.

What was this emotional abuse?

I googled it and found an article titled "27 Signs That You're Emotionally Abused."

I eagerly read the article, and to my horror, I had 26 of the 27 signs. The only one that didn't apply was the fact that I worked, but Don had been trying to get me to stop working for years.

That information was all I needed to decide that moving out was the right thing to do.

My marriage to Donald lasted ten years, twice as long as I'd expected.

Chapter Eight

'Malcolm Devoe'

After every devastating divorce, there was always a rebound relationship that took place. Divorce number three was no exception. I began my post-divorce life before I was officially divorced.

I met Malcom at a birthday party.

He was tall, dark, and athletic. Malcolm was also a mason, a fraternity member, and was ten years younger than me.

"We can never be more than friends," I said to him one day during a conversation. He wanted to take our relationship to the next level.

"Why not?" He asked impatiently.

"Among other things, you're married, and so am I." I pointed out.

"But you're about to get divorced," he reminded me. "Don't you love me?"

"I do," I admitted. "But that's not why we can't be together."

Malcom was in the military. Not only was he married, but his wife had just given birth to their third child. As a matter of fact, the night I met him, his baby boy was just two weeks old. Even if he divorced his wife, I didn't think I could live with the fact that I was the reason three children would be without their dad. I knew that pain all too well and didn't wish it on any person.

"Is it me?" He asked with an uncertainty that I recognized.

Malcom was just as insecure as I was. At the time, I didn't understand it. He was fit, and he reminded me of the guy who played on Tyler Perry's show, *Meet the Browns* - you know the one who was chocolate and fine.

"In a way, it is," I admitted. I didn't want to have to compete with all the women who would want his attention. I knew I couldn't measure up. Just wearing his Army fatigues seemed to be a 'come get me' sign to women. I'd gotten a taste of it already. Women wouldn't even acknowledge that I was standing next to him. "You're just too much work."

His feelings were hurt.

"So, I'm not worth the work?" He said.

"Yes, you are," I said more to soothe his feelings than because I believed it.

We had fun, and I loved the attention he showered on me, but I didn't believe it could be more. There were just too many obstacles.

It turns out, Malcolm's wife was sick and needed his insurance.

It was just one more reason why the two of us wouldn't work.

I didn't want that guilt on my plate.

For all the reasons not to be with him, there was only one that caused me to throw caution to the wind; I loved him.

Malcolm told me how beautiful I was. We would dress alike and attend events, and he'd hold my hand and tell people I was his woman. I had never had as much attention as he gave me.

Wasn't his attentiveness an indication that he loved me?

Love is what I'd wanted my whole life. I'd wanted to belong someplace and to someone. So, I took a gamble on love.

For a time, Malcolm and I got to have our cake and eat it too, but soon time ran out, and he was being sent to his next post in North Carolina.

He and I had hard choices to make.

Ultimately, I didn't get to choose. Malcom's wife chose for me.

Malcolm had offered her the opportunity to come to North Carolina. He wouldn't live with her but would live with me while maintaining a home for her and their children.

As sick as she was and as much as she needed him, she had enough self-worth to turn him down.

So, by default, I became the chosen one.

In May of 2013, I quit my job, left my family, and moved to Fayetteville, North Carolina.

Malcom had gone out ahead of me to check in with the Army and to find us a place to live. Because we weren't married to each other, we couldn't live on base. He found us a house not far from Fort Bragg.

I'll never forget the day I arrived.

Malcom was sitting outside, working with the movers inventorying our furniture. He saw me drive up, but instead of walking out to meet me, he just sat there. That was totally out of his character.

I had been driving for 14 hours; I was anxious and excited to see him. I got out of the car and walked up the driveway. When I got close to him, I expected he would pull me into his arms and welcome me with a kiss. He didn't.

"Hi," I said. "I made it."

"Hey," he said. "I see."

We stood there awkwardly. Then, finally, he spoke again. "Listen, I got to get back to work. Can you finish this for me?"

"Sure," I said as I turned away so he wouldn't see the tears in my eyes. "Let me use the bathroom first."

I went inside and found the restroom. When I came out, he was already gone. I stood there in the driveway alone, wondering what I'd gotten myself into.

Being home alone became the norm. Malcom left before the sun rose and made it home most nights well past 10 pm. For all intents and purposes, I was on my own.

I'd never lived anywhere alone before. It was daunting, and I was completely devastated.

I didn't have a job, but I'd cashed in my 401K. After 15 years of service, it was a nice amount. I paid off all my bills, put some in savings, and decided to live off the rest until I found a job I *wanted*.

While I waited, I enrolled in school and began writing. I also found a life coach. I decided that I would put all my free time to good use.

The more I worked on me, the further apart Malcom and I grew. We began to argue routinely. He would bring up stuff that I'd long since forgotten, and I was caught off guard. He had led me to believe that the best thing about us was our ability to communicate. It turned out that he'd been hiding his true feelings.

"Why are you doing this?" I asked, crying harder than I ever had before. Malcom was my last opportunity to get it right. I had given him all I had, but it still hadn't been enough.

"Don't act like you don't know what's going on?" Malcom said viciously. "I gave up everything for you. I left my family."

"I gave up things too," I said.

"Your children are grown," he said with an emptiness I didn't recognize. "It's not the same."

"So you're saying my love for my children isn't the same as yours?" I asked incredulously.

"I'm saying you got the opportunity to raise your kids," he said in a condescending tone.

"Malcolm, this was your idea," I reminded him.

"I can't help how I feel," he said with a coldness that penetrated my bones. "I don't know what you want from me."

The conversation went downhill from there. We both said things that we shouldn't have and maybe didn't mean, but they were out there. He left and came back, but even more angry than when he'd left. For most of the night, we just argued without any resolution in sight.

"I just want security," I cried, feeling warm liquid pour down my legs. I was so upset; I'd peed my pants. Then a weird thing happened. As I shouted out to him, a realization came over me. I had a clarity I'd never had before.

This man could never give me what I was asking for.

As a matter of fact, I was now certain that no person or thing on this earth could ever fill the hole in my soul.

I moved out of Malcolm's house while he was away at on drill. I knew he'd be hurt, but I also knew I would never be able to leave while he was here. So, I took what felt like the coward's way out and did it while he was away.

Although I left his home, I didn't leave the state. I wasn't ready to give up completely.

A few weeks later, Malcom had his children come out for the summer. Before I'd moved out, I had promised him that I would keep them while he worked. I felt it was important to keep my word. So, every morning I would come over to his house before he left. I made him breakfast; then, I made breakfast and lunch for the kids. Some days I made dinner, but often, he would come home early enough to make them dinner.

I wondered why he had never been able to make it home much for dinner when I'd lived there.

He treated me so cold. No one would have guessed we were ever in love. He talked to his children, but not me, and when he did speak to me, it was like he was talking to a stranger. As cold as he was towards me, he didn't want me to leave.

It was the oddest thing. I felt like he was demanding me to stay and take his punishment.

"I'm going to leave now," I said, grabbing my purse one evening after he'd gotten home. I wasn't interested in hanging around for the cold, silent treatment.

"Why?" he asked with a clear attitude. "Don't you want to stay and have dinner with us? The kids want you to stay."

So, I stayed, but it was sheer torture. Then, after dinner, he encouraged me to stay overnight.

"You may as well stay," he said. "That way, you won't have to get up so early."

He phrased it like he was concerned for me, so I was fooled. And again, it was torturous.

The kids slept in the beds upstairs. His oldest slept in the king-sized bed I'd left behind because my apartment was too small for the bed.

I wondered where Malcom and I were going to sleep.

Malcom pulled out an air mattress and blew it up. As I watched it expand, I felt my heart sink. This man, who had once put me on a pedestal, now treated me as if I were any old person off the street.

Tears blurred my vision, but I didn't have the courage to leave. A part of me felt guilty like I deserved this treatment. After all, it had been my choice to leave.

As we laid on the air mattress, there was enough space between us for another person. I longed for him to touch me, not because I craved sex, but because I craved intimacy. I didn't want him to be mad at me. I wanted him to talk to me, and it was driving me mad that he wouldn't.

The silent treatment was the worst thing I'd ever experienced. Maybe it was because it reminded me of all the times Mama had used that as her weapon of choice.

I endured that treatment for the rest of the summer, and when the kids left, I decided to leave as well.

But again, Malcom convinced me to stay.

"So, you just gonna leave me out here by myself?" He asked irritated.

"But why do you want me to stay?" I asked confused more than ever. "You don't talk to me or want to touch me."

"You are the one who moved out," he shouted. "And now you just gonna leave me all alone."

Out of guilt, I stayed.

The apartment I'd rented had gas heat. The money I'd saved had begun to run out quicker now that I was maintaining a separate residence. I was spending twice as much as I'd budgeted. I couldn't afford to have the heat turned on. Winter came, and I'd never been so cold. Groceries were low, too, as I tried to spend wisely in order to pay my rent.

At night, I would pile blankets and comforters on my bed in an effort to stay warm. At first, I used the oven for heat, but I caught a glimpse of fire one day which scared me, so I never did that again.

By November 2014, I couldn't take it anymore.

I found a moving company and maxed out my credit card for the move.

I didn't know which was colder - the North Carolina weather or Malcolm's attitude.

Chapter Nine

'The Prophetess'

As hard as it was living in North Carolina, something awakened in me while I was there.

The place seemed to be a Mecca for art, poetry, literature, and music. I quickly caught the bug, too, and accepted an intern position at a publishing company. I was in Heaven.

As I walked into the office, my creativity stirred right away.

There was so much activity. People were coming in and calling, each and every one of them talked about books and writing.

It was glorious.

My boss, Sarah, was a walking story herself. And I guess if I'm honest, so are most creative people. The drama just seems to follow us.

Sarah had mysterious meetings and hush-hush conversations. The people she knew were scandalous, and she seemed to revel in it.

"Girl, this is what I'd do," Sarah was on the phone having a loud conversation again. "I'd buy some of that International Delight coffee creamer, pull off the label, and stick it on his windshield."

She had just been told by one of her clients that she'd read a message from her husband's mistress thanking him for an afternoon of delight.

I shook my head.

We had way too much work to do for that soap opera mess. I wasn't interested. It wasn't funny to me. I'd been on both sides of that kind of story, and there was nothing *delightful* about it.

As a matter of fact, Sarah had too. She was rumored to have had a scandal that had been taken public.

This made me even more curious as to *why* she would entertain that kind of gossip.

Not soon after I arrived in Fayetteville, I had to find someone to do my hair. I drove around and stopped in a few shops, but none struck me as any place I wanted to be.

At the last place I went to, I found a postcard advertising a book about The Proverbs 31 Woman. I wasn't really sure what that was, but the author's face looked friendly. She was offering life coaching sessions. I went home to call her. That same evening, we were sitting in a coffee shop talking about her life coaching business.

That's what I needed. I decided.

I purchased her workbook, paid for the 8-week course, and went back home to begin reading. While I was there, she'd also told me about the beauty shop she attended.

I was thrilled.

I called and made an appointment with the shop owner. Then, I began reading the workbook to prepare for the next class.

There was a chapter on pornography and masturbation. When I learned that masturbation was a sin, I was shocked and very disappointed. Malcolm's late hours left me alone so much; I'd taken to taking care of business on my own.

Now what?

I put down the workbook, picked up a pen, and began writing. When I was done, it was as if I'd been in some sort of trance. It was all about the Book of Acts. I wasn't a Bible scholar, and I had no idea how I knew what I'd written! I turned it around in my head for a while, then finally closed my laptop and went to bed.

The next day, I had an appointment with the new hairstylist. I liked her right of way. She was larger than life, full of giggles, and absolutely gorgeous.

The first thing she did was give me a hug, and I nearly burst into tears.

"You're beautiful," she said, and it was as if she somehow knew I needed some love. "What can I do for you?"

"I don't know," I said hesitantly. As I looked around the shop, the hairstyles were bold, colorful, fun, and free. "I want to be free too."

She laughed and said, "Honey, don't we all."

Hours later, as I sat under the dryer, she sat next to me and handed me a sliver of paper.

"God told me to give you this," she said as I took the paper.

When I read it, my mouth flew open.

"What is it?" She asked.

"I just wrote this last night," I said full of bewilderment.

She laughed. "Well, I just do what I'm told."

Later, when I sat in her chair, she said, "So you're a ghostwriter, huh?"

I didn't know what that was, but I nodded my head. If there was anything I was sure about, it was my love for writing and writing's love for me. I could look at anything, and instead of seeing what was there, I saw how it should be. If words were out of place, they quickly came into subjection under my watchful eye.

When I got home, I googled ghostwriting and was shocked. There was the term for what

I'd been doing for as long as I could remember.

Had God brought me all the way to North Carolina to show me my purpose?

It turned out that the stylist was also a Prophetess!

I didn't know what that was either until she told me. I was skeptical at first, but I knew better than to speak on it one way or the other. So, I watched her to see what she did with this "so-called" gift from God.

I never saw her exploit it. She wasn't holding seances. She would just say things gently, and if you weren't paying attention, you would just call it encouragement.

Still, I decided I wasn't going to ask her anything, mostly because I didn't want to know any bad news. My plate was full, and I didn't have room for anything more.

I believe Prophetess knew that (of course she did), and she never gave me anything bad. But what she did give me was confidence. The things she said to me came to pass, and soon, I had no doubts about her.

The funny thing is that once she started telling me things, God sent other people to confirm. At one point, three different people from three different corners of the world told me the same thing.

I was told that I would be married within five years of moving back to Arkansas, and the man would be "crazy" about me.

I was also told that I'd have multiple homes, one being a cabin in Utah or Colorado, where I'd go to write.

And I was also told that I'd have a book signing and that the people would be in a line wrapped about the building waiting for me to sign their book.

Chapter Ten

'Starting Over, Again'

Even though most of the things the Prophetess said came to pass, I still had my doubts.

Why would God do all of those things for me? All I'd ever done for Him was mess up. Was I even worthy?

I had grown weary, and I needed to know that it was going to be alright. I needed to know that all the pain I'd endured would somehow be worth it in the end. Prophetess words offered hope that it would all work out in the end. I tried hard to hold on to them.

I returned to Arkansas with much less than I had when I left – emotionally and financially. I was broke and broken.

Back in Arkansas, life felt weird. Life had gone on without me.

Nothing looked or felt the same. The world moved on without me, and there was no trace of me ever being here.

People I once called friends were now strangers. I felt like I didn't belong anywhere. I felt isolated and alone.

My apartment wasn't ready when I arrived, so for several weeks, I lived with my daughter. One day I looked down at my keyring and realized the only key on it was my car key. I was homeless for the first time in my life.

How did I get here?

Christmas came too soon, and I had nothing. Although my children were grown, I felt like such a failure because I couldn't buy them anything. I desperately wanted to give up and cry, but I didn't have any place private to do that. I kept on a brave face and kept getting out of bed every day.

Somehow, I made it through the holiday season and moved into my apartment.

As happy as I was to be in my own place, it was the first time in my life that I lived all alone.

At night I slept on the sofa, with all the lights on, so I could see the front door. After hours of lying awake, I would finally fall asleep from sheer exhaustion.

Then, after years of holding it all in, the crying started.

And what I'd always feared would happen, happened. I started crying and couldn't stop.

At first, I thought I was crying over Malcom.

Why am I crying so much over this man? I wondered.

It wasn't the first time my heart had been broken, and it wasn't the first time I was disappointed by love.

Although I'd left Malcolm in North Carolina, like all of my relationships, I'd been abandoned long before the relationship ended. Malcom hadn't been an exception.

Truthfully, he had never been with me. It turned out that what we had was just a story I'd made up. He hadn't been honest, and we hadn't really communicated. All along, I'd been talking to myself because he only repeated the things that he knew I wanted to hear.

One day while in the shower, the reason I was crying so much and why it seemed I'd never get over Malcom was revealed to me:

For the first time in my life, there was no distraction from my pain. I wasn't dating anyone. There was no rebound man. So, now I was not only grieving my relationship with Malcom; finally I was grieving all the other broken relationships in my life - including my relationship with Mama. And the loss of Mr. Jack.

Mama had said that crying cleans your eyes. As the crying subsided, my vision became clear.

Every relationship I'd ever had seem to have been with people who weren't available to me for one reason or another. Abandonment had happened to me too many times to be a coincidence:

I had learned that my first love, Benny Pete, had indeed been seeing Dora Kellogg.

Edward Carlson had a girl pregnant when he got me pregnant.

While we were in Arizona, Bradford James had had an affair with the neighbor who babysat our son.

Anton had a wife.

William had been cheating on me with one of his lodge sisters.

Gregg had been married.

Donald had been involved with a woman in El Dorado when I met him.

And Malcolm had been married.

Why was I drawn to what was out of my reach? Was I attracted to what I thought I couldn't have?

Mama had loved and born children with Mr. Jack, who as I learned was not hers to love either.

Was this a generational curse? Why did it seem that the only people interested in me were the ones who were already taken?

I didn't want to do that anymore. I didn't want to be that girl anymore.

I sat down and made a list. It was time to have standards and to become deliberate in whom I allowed into my life.

The top things on the list were that he had to be single, available, and interested in me. It seemed simple enough.

It was time to get my life on track. Waiting for Malcom or any man to rescue me was a fantasy that had run its course.

I attempted to go back to my old life, but that door had closed, and I was forced to rely on a business I'd started while I was in North Carolina.

In January of 2014, I started a publishing company at the urging of Sarah. I hadn't gotten very far with it due to my focus on Malcom.

Maybe now was the time to do so.

In December of 2014, I published my first book. By September of that following year, I had an office space and enough clients to sustain my personal life as well as my business expenses.

One afternoon, Dr. Cleo Lions made an appointment to talk about a book she had written. Cleo was a plus-sized woman with style. She had a big voice and a big personality. I liked her. She was there to talk about publishing a children's book, but like most people who encountered me, she began to tell me her life story.

Dr. Lions said she'd met her husband when the two of them had been married to other people. After a brief affair, they decided to end things to be obedient to their faith.

"I think I'm cursed," I said flatly. "The only men who are interested in me are married or involved with someone else," I said frustrated. "So, I've decided that when I see them coming, I'm going to run in the other direction."

"Why would you do that?" She asked.

I thought that was a strange question. Dr. Cleo was also a minister. I know she knew that adultery was wrong.

"Because I don't want to be involved in sinful behavior," I said slowly, wondering if this was a test or a trick question.

"Maybe you shouldn't run," she said.

"Huh?" I asked. "Why shouldn't I?"

"Maybe the people you meet aren't there for romantic involvements," Dr. Cleo said. "Maybe they are there to point out something to you, but you're confusing that with romance."

Dr. Cleo was in and out of my life so quickly; I never got the chance to discuss her advice.

And since it didn't make much sense, I dismissed it.

Epilogue

'Going Home'

Everyone I'd ever loved had let me down in one way or another. And now, it seemed I couldn't even trust in myself. I didn't know God, so I couldn't trust Him either. I had no understanding. I had no love. I had no faith.

At rock bottom, I got an idea to try church again.

By the time I arrived at Rock Creek, I was completely overwhelmed. There was nothing in my life that was going the way I thought it should go.

I entered the church, and immediately the tears began to pour out of me. I felt like a weight was being lifted. Service was only an hour long, but I felt the desire to stay the whole day. I came back week after week, and the same thing happened.

Malcolm and I had been apart for more than two years, and I had finally decided to let go of any hope that he'd come back to get me. My apartment walls were still bare and white. I hadn't thought it was a good idea to spend time decorating because I knew he'd come to get me, but he didn't.

Why was my life so hard? Why was this happening to me?

I'd tried to do right. Even when I did wrong, it was with good intentions. There were things I didn't do because they were wrong. I wanted to live a good life. I wanted to be a good person. But it didn't seem to matter. My life was in ruins.

All around me, I saw people who weren't good people and didn't care to be. They were successful and living carefree lives.

So, why was it so hard for me?

I'd had suicidal thoughts for years, but I never told anyone. I didn't want anyone to think I was crazy. I wasn't crazy unless crazy meant too tired to keep fighting.

I was crazy if it meant wanting the hurt to stop.

I didn't know how to make it stop. I didn't know where to turn. In my life, I'd always been the strong one. I was the one that others came to for help. I had the answers for them.

How come I didn't have any for me?

Then, one day, an answer came.

Now that my children were grown and I was alone, I would end my life.

As I sat in the sanctuary, I looked around and thought, *I think these nice white people who have money will help bury me if they knew me.*

Armed with a new plan, I had renewed strength.

I attended church regularly. I met some nice people, and soon, they were saying hi to me on Sundays. They knew my name!

I joined a life group, too, and again, I met more people and began to feel connected.

I was enjoying the love I got from my church members. I even found myself wanting the kind of love I saw the people sharing with each other and their significant others. I longed for the love I saw between mother and daughter, father and daughter, and friends.

Why do you want that? I shook my head. You didn't come here for that. You came here to die.

It felt hopeful, but I had been tricked by hope before. I'd been tricked by love too. Neither ever lasted.

Soon, it was time to put my plan into action.

"Cleanliness is next to Godliness," Mama always said.

I cleaned up my apartment and put things in place. I didn't bother with a note. What could I say that would make sense?

I took a shower and oiled my body well.

"Put some lotion on them ashy legs." I was still hearing Mama's voice.

When they found me, I wanted to be clean. I didn't want to be ashy either.

I unlocked my apartment door, so they wouldn't have to break the deadbolt. I went into the kitchen and poured a tall glass of water.

Without hesitation, I took a handful of muscle relaxers and drank the entire glass of water.

I turned out the lights, got into bed, pulled the covers up to my neck, and laid there waiting for sleep to come. I knew that with sleep, would come peace.

This would be a secret I wouldn't have to keep.

Book III

Faith In God

For Mama and Me and Mine.

My Father

In losing my father, I lost my way.

There was no joy in any day.

And so, began my search for a new love,

the kind that's so close and fits like a glove.

My intentions were good, and my need was strong.

I looked everywhere on Earth, each place being wrong.

Years went by, and oh, how many times I cried.

Peace and love escaped me, no matter how hard I tried.

I began to ask God, "Why," because it didn't seem fair.

Then, I remembered Job and wondered how could I dare,

question the Lord or ask for a reason.

He has said for all things there is a time and a season.

I almost gave up but decided on one last try.

That's when I reached out to the One who sits most high.

He answered my prayers, as He promised He would.

He filled my soul with love as only He could.

Now, I have hope, peace, and love,

from my Father – Jesus, who loves me from above.

Iris M. Williams

10/17/2015

Foreword

Mama used to say, "You need to know the Lord for yo' self."

At the time, I had no idea what she meant. Later I learned she was saying that we should all have an individual relationship with God. She was right.

For most of my life, I allowed others to determine my worth, what I said (or didn't say), and even what I did (or didn't do). I gave my power away and silenced my voice.

If I'd had the knowledge or the courage, I'd have told Dr. Buckhead that a torn hymen didn't mean I'd had sex. I'd have told him that the discharge in my panties was likely due to the antibiotics I'd taken over the years after having multiple surgeries (13 by the time I was 13) on my hip.

Because I didn't know these things, I couldn't stand up for myself. I guess Mama didn't know either.

That encounter with Dr. Buckhead began a lifetime of accepting the conclusions of others. I let Dr. Buckhead define me. Mama defined me, and there were many others after them who picked up where the two of them left off.

I read somewhere that if you don't stand for something, you'll fall for anything. I had no standards, so I believed and fell for everything.

When people showed me who they were, I didn't dare to reconcile it with what they were saying. I'd been told I was ignorant, so I allowed that to define me. I took for granted that maybe I just misunderstood what I was seeing or hearing. I didn't trust my judgment.

It's taken me 50 years, but finally, I can see me. I see the flaws, but more than that, I see the me God intended, and I'm far more precious than rubies.

Now, I can live an abundant life.

Iris M. Williams

Acknowledgment

I thank God for Jesus and the Holy Spirit. I am thankful for wisdom and discernment.

Some time ago, I sat in my office, and from my window, I watched a bird.

It was FAT (cared for)! I had never seen such a FAT bird, but then it flew up and back down. It was also agile.

The bird sat still, in the moment, watching and waiting. Then, quickly, it moved and turned around completely. And just like that, its circumstance and vantage point changed.

I am that bird, FAT (cared for), standing still, waiting for my circumstance to change – quickly, completely.

I believe.

To God be the Glory.

Prologue

I enjoyed the love I got from my church members. I even found myself wanting the kind of love I saw people sharing with their significant others. I longed for the love I saw between mother and daughter, father and daughter, man and wife, and friends.

Why do you want that? I shook my head. You didn't come here for that. You came here to die.

I felt hopeful, but I had been tricked by hope before. I'd been tricked by love too. Neither ever lasted.

Soon, it was time to put my plan into action.

Cleanliness is next to Godliness.

Mama's words were never far from my mind. I cleaned up my apartment and put things in place. I didn't bother with a note. What could I say that would make sense?

I took a shower and oiled my body well.

Put some lotion on them ashy legs.

Again, Mama's voice interrupted my thoughts.

When they found me, I wanted to be clean. I didn't want to be ashy either.

I unlocked my apartment door, so they wouldn't have to break the deadbolt. I went into the kitchen and poured a tall glass of water.

Without hesitation, I took a handful of muscle relaxers and drank the entire glass of water.

I turned out the lights, got into bed, pulled the covers up to my neck, and laid there waiting for sleep to come. I knew that with sleep, would come peace.

This would be a secret I wouldn't have to keep.

Introduction

'Faith in God'

I woke up coughing and scared. The important thing is, I woke up – in more ways than one. I awakened to the realization that it wasn't my time to go. For whatever reason, God wanted me to live.

Since I knew my answer wasn't in the world, I focused on what wasn't of this world. It was time I tried God.

Who was He? Who was I? Why was I here?

Something told me that the peace I was seeking would be found in the answers to those questions.

I continued to attend The Church at Rock Creek. *Something* also told me that answers to my questions would be found there.

One Sunday, an ad in the worship guide caught my attention. It was an ad for a part-time position in the church. *Something* whispered, "That's your job."

After service, I sat in my car in the parking lot and called the number listed. I left a voice message, and by the next day, I was sitting in Pastor Garvin's office listening to him talk about Jesus.

"Tell me about your journey, Iris."

I opened my mouth, and my heart fell out.

"I went in search of me and found Christ," I said with conviction. "I've realized that what I need can't be found in a person or things. What I need can only be gained by having a personal relationship with Jesus."

Talking with Pastor Garvin was easy. He listened and seemed genuinely interested. He hired me on the spot.

Instead of my office being at the main church where Pastor Garvin's office and the Tuesday night Celebrate Recovery meetings were held, I was placed in the Care Center, which was headquarters for the Church's food bank.

Was this some cruel joke?

My finances had been strained since I returned from North Carolina. I was literally living on faith. On paper, my life didn't add up, yet month after month, things worked out.

I was living on a shoestring budget and sacrificing nonessentials for the necessities. Most days, I only ate once. Needless to say, sitting in the food bank aggravated my stomach.

I drank all the free coffee I could stand, trying to dull the rumblings that I didn't want anyone to hear and focused on my work.

One of my duties was to provide food for the attendees of the Celebrate Recovery group Pastor Garvin led on Tuesday nights. So, at least once a week, I ate at least twice. While there were usually leftovers, I never took any. I didn't want to be greedy, or maybe the truth is, I didn't want anyone to know that I needed help.

As I scrambled with keeping my dignity, Mary, who was over the food bank, came to my desk one day and handed me a card.

"Here is this card," she said tentatively. "You can get food once a month. And today, I want you to come and get all the produce you want. We got in a huge shipment, and we'll never be able to give it all away. I don't want it to go to waste."

I didn't dare say anything for fear of bursting into tears. I just nodded my head and whispered, "Thank you."

After saying a quick prayer of thanks, I got up and went to the freezer. I smiled. God doesn't just send random blessings, His blessings are tailormade for us individually.

The things in the freezer were things I'd wanted to buy, and here I was able to get as much of it as I wanted for free.

I took what I needed and didn't overindulge.

For months, that's how I ate.

In addition to the food bank, God sent people to bless me more by inviting me to lunch or dinner.

At first, I declined the invitations because I didn't have extra money for eating out. So, instead of telling the truth, I declined with the excuse of work. I did work. As a matter of fact, I worked day and night.

But then the phone calls and text messages from my friends began with, "I know you're busy, but …"

I realized I was sacrificing my new friends because of my pride. I didn't want that to happen. These were people who loved me even though I had nothing to offer them material wise. They were important to me.

I never wanted people to think of me as 'too busy' for them. I knew spending time with friends and family was important.

Something said, "Just say yes." sometimes and be smart with what I ordered. To my surprise, the person I met with would generally insist on paying. And on the occasion when I paid, I had extra money. God worked it out.

I know this was just another way God was caring for me. He always gave me more than I asked for and more than I needed.

The more He did, the more I desired an intimate relationship with Him. I wanted to know more about Him. Before working for the church, I'd looked into organized Bible courses. They were expensive, and I didn't have the money for them.

"Oh, and I don't know if you'd be interested in this or not," Pastor Garvin said one week in our staff meeting, "but we encourage our staff to attend Downline if their schedule permits."

Downline was a discipleship course that taught the Bible from Genesis to Revelation. It focused on how to read the Bible, explained the job of a disciple, and offered practical instruction on how to be an effective disciple. God was answering yet another prayer!

I learned so much. Until that class, I had always thought that salvation was about me and only me. Now I knew that our lives are about pointing others to Christ.

Downline was what I *wanted*, and our Tuesday night Celebrate Recovery meetings were what I *needed*.

Once a week, I sat in Small Group listening to people release their hurts in hopes of gaining freedom. I appreciated their bravery and candor. I understood that I wasn't alone. I also was reassured that just because you choose to live for Christ doesn't guarantee you a trouble-free life.

Actually, the opposite is true.

One night, a young woman showed up and shared her testimony. It broke my heart.

"It's been a year now since my mother committed suicide," she said through tears. "But I can't get past the pain. I feel like it just happened yesterday."

I cried with her as I realized my plan might have ended my pain, but it would only transfer it to the people I said I loved the most.

How could I have peace knowing I'd leave a legacy of pain?

So, I determined to live.

I surrendered my life to God and accepted whatever would come my way. I stopped worrying so much about money and decided that if God can take care of the birds, He can surely provide for me. The Bible says so!

I had already hit rock bottom, and all I had left was belief. So, I decided to live it.

For years, I had been under the false assumption that the only person I could count on was me. But after years of making one bad decision after another, it seems I couldn't even count on me either.

I'd put faith in others only to be disappointed.

I'd put faith in myself only to be let down.

It was time to place my faith in the One who made me.

It was time to put faith in God.

Chapter One: SAD

'Love Never Forgets'

After my third divorce, I began to feel overwhelmed with emotional baggage. Everyone around me was taking some pill or another (Xanax, Zoloft, etc.), and I thought I'd go and get me a pill, and things would be ok.

There is something that happens when you take a pill for a disorder you don't have.

Instead of being sad, I became angry. When I found myself very upset because someone parked next to me in the parking deck at work, I knew pills weren't going to be the answer I'd been seeking.

I visited Dr. Google and stumbled upon a diagnosis I thought sounded perfect.

Seasonal Affective Disorder is the diagnosis given to people whose moods change based on the season.

I thought I had it. I was researching lamps and medications to rid myself of the overwhelming, nearly crippling sadness that came over me as soon as the summer season gave way to fall and winter.

But lamps and pills didn't work.

Finally, I pushed past the stereotypical ethnic barriers (black people don't go to therapy) and got in counseling.

"I don't know why I'm so sad," I told my therapist.

Dr. Patricia Stone operated a clinic in a renovated home in North Little Rock. I felt comfortable there because it really did seem like I was entering someone's cozy home instead of a cold, sterile doctor's office.

"Do you have any idea why?" she asked.

One thing I learned about therapists is they were advocates for getting YOU to talk. Initially, going to therapy felt like a waste of money since I did most of the talking. I wanted her to 'fix me' or 'tell me what to do.' That's not how it works at all.

"No," I answered. "I just know that every year, this happens. At first, I thought it was because of whatever relationship I was in or had just ended. Then, I thought it was the weather."

"And you don't think that now?" She asked.

"No," I said and sighed. I felt like she knew what was wrong but was wanting me to get to that ah-ha moment on my own.

"So, tell me how you feel besides sadness."

I thought about it for a moment. I hadn't taken the time to analyze what all I was feeling. I stopped at being sad.

"Well, I feel helpless and weak and even afraid," I began surprising myself at what I was saying.

Why hadn't I thought about this before?

"Did something traumatic happen to you during the fall or winter season?" She asked, looking directly at me over the rim of her glasses.

Suddenly feeling uncomfortable, I shifted in my seat. Memories of placing my son for adoption came flooding back in a rush. The day I left the hospital, it was cold, dark, and (ding ding ding) it was winter.

For years, I'd tried to forget about that day.

But no matter what my mind did, my heart refused to move on past that day.

"Yes," I managed to say, blinking back tears. "I placed a child up for adoption."

I told Dr. Stone how I'd gotten pregnant at 15, how my Mama had taken my baby, moved out of state with her, and later that year in the winter of 1987, I'd given birth to a baby boy. I'd kept the second pregnancy secret from everyone who knew me. Feeling like I had no choice, I'd given my baby boy up for adoption.

"Do you know what happened to your baby?"

"Only what my social worker told me," I confessed. "She was sending me pictures, but eventually we lost touch. I couldn't bear to see him anymore."

I felt horrible for losing touch on purpose.

Was I a monster for not wanting to know?

"So, how long has it been?"

"In the last photos, he was probably eight," I confessed.

"So, he's a grown man now?"

My son was over the age of 21 by this time, but in my mind, he'd forever be that sweet, tiny baby with a head full of black hair and big beautiful brown eyes.

Dr. Stone stood up and handed me a box of Kleenex. I hadn't been aware that I was crying.

"Iris, you don't *have* SAD," she began. "You *are* sad. But you've been pretending like you aren't. Your body is responding to what your mind refuses to acknowledge."

Suddenly, it all made sense.

I'd been trying to forget someone who was a part of me.

Love never leaves.

Iris M. Williams

It also won't be ignored.

Chapter Two: Purpose

'Writing Saved My Life'

Right before I left North Carolina in 2014, Maya Angelou died. When I learned she'd been just up the road from me in Winston, Salem, I was distraught.

On the day of the funeral, I was home alone as usual. The service was broadcast live on television. I thought about driving up to Winston, Salem, but realized I'd never get inside the church. At least if I watched it at home, I could see and hear more than I would if I were there having to sit or stand outside.

As I stood in the middle of the living room floor, I cried as if she were my mother, friend, sister, or auntie, because she was. We were connected.

From the moment I'd read her book, "I Know Why the Caged Bird Sings," I'd felt a kindred spirit with Maya.

The similarities of our lives were too many to ignore:

She was molested as a child, so was I.

She had to recite an Easter poem and couldn't, so did I (the same poem too).

She was raised in a small town by an older woman, so was I.

Maya lost her voice due to trauma, so did I. (Not literally, but figuratively in that I allowed others to dictate my life.)

Maya loved writing, and so did I.

But as much as we were alike, we were also worlds apart.

Maya had a mother who talked to her and doted on her. I did not.

Maya had a brother who loved and protected her. I did not.

When Maya decided to speak, people listened. People rarely paid attention to me.

Maya traveled, loved, and was fearless. I was stuck, unloved, and fearful.

In spite of our differences and because of our similarities, I loved her, and I held on to the belief that if she'd known me, maybe she'd have loved me too. I hoped.

I missed out on an opportunity to be loved.

After Maya's funeral, there were so many articles and news stories on her. I read them all, but I couldn't get enough. I began reading and listening to hear autobiographies and was shocked at what I'd learned.

For all her greatness, Maya had done things like everyone else, including making bad choices.

When I found out that she'd had multiple marriages and divorces like me, I was stunned and full of questions.

As I hungrily read, I found myself wishing she'd talked about more about her failed relationships. But even when asked, she was elusive. Maybe, the one thing Maya hadn't done was overcome the societal shame of multiple marriages.

Why else would she not talk about it?

Surely, she had to know how important a subject it was. Was it shame?

I could certainly understand shame. For years, I refused to talk about my multiple divorces. Like my secret pregnancy and subsequent adoption, shame was a sore subject that was better left in a closet with other skeletal remains of a life unlived.

I was ashamed of my marriages and divorces, and yet the irony of the situation wasn't lost on me. Society had a funny way of choosing what things were taboo.

Apparently, it's not shameful to have a new sex partner every few months or to be in a loveless marriage while cheating; however, to have multiple marriages and divorces - something *had* to be wrong with you!

And while something was wrong with me (bad choices and failing to acknowledge my pain), I wasn't the worse person in the world. I wasn't damaged goods.

So, why did I feel that way? Why was it hard to reconcile what I felt with what I kenw?

After listening to Maya's stories and not understanding why she didn't write about her relationship failures extensively as she did most other things, I remembered something I'd heard once.

"If what you want isn't available, then that just means you need to create it."

Did that mean I needed to write my story?

But my story began long before I was married or divorced.

Was there a connection?

I tried, but my attempts were futile. Writing about my pain meant dealing with my pain, and that was something I couldn't bring myself to do.

So, I hired a ghostwriter, and once again, I handed off something precious to me for a total stranger to nourish.

After paying a hefty fee and doing extensive interviews for more than a year, she finally told me she couldn't write it, and she didn't know why.

I knew why.

The story wasn't hers to write. I needed to write it.

Finally, I decided to sit down, and you guessed it, freedom visited me.

When I was done writing, I did something I hadn't done before. I read what I'd written. Guess what I found? Patterns!

I saw the same things happen over and over. The people and places were different, but the scenarios were all the same.

I was sad for the little girl who was betrayed. I hurt for the lost teenager. I rolled my eyes at the foolish young adult. I grieved for them all.

I realized the things I'd allowed and had done were in retaliation and were a feeble attempt at self-preservation.

As a mother, grandmother, wife, and friend, I found empathy for myself and began to forgive myself for the ignorance.

I knew I had to love Iris to love others, but I also had to learn to receive love. The first person I had to receive love from was me.

I began to work at getting to know Iris. Without a husband, boyfriend or children to care for, I had time to get to know me. With work and time, I decided that I liked this Iris person, and with a little work, I could even love her.

Self-discovery. It's amazing.

I'd been writing long before I discovered Maya or North Carolina, but my encounter with her after she passed caused me to be more intentional with my writing. I wanted to do for someone else what Maya's biographies had done for me.

I wanted to pay it forward.

If writing could save my life, I knew it could do the same for someone else.

Chapter Three: Life

'A Tribute'

I had only been publishing three years when a friend of mine sent Addy to me. She said she'd been working on a manuscript for several years and was finally finished, but she didn't know what to do with it.

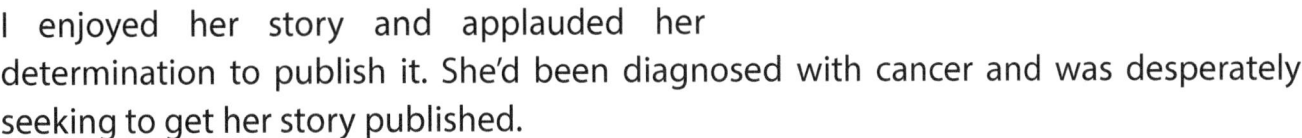

Her story was well developed and was kind of unusual for me as it took place on board a navy ship. Addy was ex-military and had been involved in an abusive relationship.

I enjoyed her story and applauded her determination to publish it. She'd been diagnosed with cancer and was desperately seeking to get her story published.

"Everyone who knows my story has told me that I need to publish it," Addy said in a voice that was strained. She sounded like a raspy-voiced blues singer. I felt her heart over the telephone and liked her right away.

I sent her some forms, she sent me her manuscript, and our relationship began.

During the editing process, I go back and forth with the authors quite a bit. Addy's work was no exception. This was the part I liked the most because I got to know the authors intimately - if they're open to it, and most of them are.

Generally, I'm the first person who actively listens to them about their life and their book.

Overwhelmingly, many authors find themselves opening up to me not only about their books but about their personal lives as well. They tell me their secrets.

Addy was always so pleasant and agreeable. She trusted me completely with her work, and that just made me want to give and do all that I could give and do.

"I'm not sure I'm going to make it to see my book published, Ms. Iris," Addy said one day.

My heart went out to her, and I immediately thought of my brother, Alphonso, who had died from complications of prostate cancer in 2013.

What was it about the thought of death that pushed people to live?

Alphonso's death reminded me that time is not on our side. There is not always tomorrow.

"It will get published," I assured her. I would make sure of that. "Let's just focus on today and what needs to happen."

I tried to be encouraging — most of what I said or wanted to say sounded cliché to me.

How could I reassure anyone of anything?

I didn't have answers for my own life and surely didn't have any for anyone else. I had just as many questions about life and death as Addy did - if not more.

Addy had terminal cancer, and yet, I found myself envying her.

She had a loving husband who adored her. She and her son were best friends, and she was close to her family. For me, that was everything.

Addy's book released, and she had a hugely successful book signing. She sent me pictures, and her face was all aglow with her achievement. I longed to be there, but finances and work took precedence.

"I'll make sure I attend the next one for your sequel," I promised.

But it was a promise I wouldn't get to keep.

It was time to send royalty reports and payments. I was so excited for Addy to see how well her book had been doing. I waited eagerly for her call or email. I sent emails and called her, but she didn't respond.

I was so busy; I didn't bother to investigate.

Then, one day, the friend who referred her called me.

"Iris," he began. "You heard about Addy, didn't you?"

My heart sank, and I sat back in my seat.

"No," I responded in a small voice. "I've been trying to reach her, but ..."

"She passed," he said.

He was trying to say more, but it was too much.

"Wait," I cried. "Wait. Wait. Wait. No, not yet."

The tears were unexpected, and they gushed out of me in waves. I felt like I couldn't breathe. I felt out of control and run over.

What was happening?

"I'll call you back," he said. I'm sure he didn't expect that reaction from me. "I'll call you back to check on you."

I sat and cried like a baby.

How was it that I could cry for this woman whom I'd never met, but not for my father? How could I weep and mourn for a lady who was not related to me, but I barely shed a tear for my brother? What was wrong with me?

Looking back on that time, I think it was the beginning of a physical metamorphosis. A mental metamorphosis had begun when I left North Carolina. Now, my body was responding to what my mind was saying.

Was it finally time (and OK) to grieve?

Chapter Four: Standards

'A Woman's Worth'

After my breakup with Malcolm, I decided celibacy was the route I wanted to take. I also decided I didn't want a romantic relationship. Since all my heartbreaks had one thing in common - me, I needed time to figure out what was going on.

I had been guilty of giving too much too soon to the wrong people. And I'd run out of gas. I was empty and had nothing left to give.

I felt myself turning into an angry black woman, and I didn't like how that looked on me.

If you ever want to test your resolve, announce what you won't do.

"Hey, Iris," Earl said. "I see that you're back in Little Rock. You want to go grab some dinner?"

I had known Earl since I was in first grade. By default, I trusted him. He had a full-time job but was also pursuing a dream. I felt that maybe he could understand the demands in my life.

"Sure," I said hesitantly but excited. I wondered if I should tell him about my decision to be celibate. But once again, fear took over, and I remained silent.

"You pick the restaurant," he said. "And you can have whatever you want!"

"Wow," I said, feeling impressed. "It's like that, hunh?"

I was considerate of his coins and decided upon Bonefish Grill. It wasn't a cheap restaurant, but I generally ordered off the appetizer menu anyway, so it would be fine.

We met, talked, and had quite a bit in common. I was hopeful that this would lead to 'something.'

"So, who are you dating these days," he asked. "I know a beautiful woman like you has to have a man."

"Thanks," I said, flattered over the compliment. This was a man who could have any woman, and yet, he'd chosen to pursue me. That did good things for my confidence. "But I'm single and not dating. Taking some time to get to know me."

"I never understood why people say that," Earl replied. "Haven't you lived with yourself long enough to know who you are?"

"That makes sense," I said cautiously. In addition to giving my body too soon, I'd also been guilty of giving my thoughts and emotions too soon as well. Along with holding out on sex, I'd decided not to talk too much. "But, it's not always the case, I guess."

There was plenty more I could have added, like the reason I didn't know myself is because I'd always became the person with whom I was in a relationship with. I liked and did whatever they wanted me to like and do. So, no, I didn't have a clue who I was. But Earl didn't need to know that. I'd learned that some people take what you say and feed it back to you. I knew what I thought and wanted. I wanted to know what he thought and wanted. I wanted to get to know him, and I wanted him to know me too. Then, together, we could decide how far to take this thing.

"I heard that women know within minutes of meeting a man if she'll sleep with him," he said and laughed. Then, he leaned closer to me and whispered, "So, am I coming back to your place after dinner?"

Any hopes I had for an 'us' quickly evaporated. It was the same old thing I'd always gotten. I was disappointed, but I was also feeling a new feeling.

I felt powerful!

I saw this as a disaster waiting to happen, and I was determined to walk away from it before I got hurt. I wasn't going to give him any part of me.

"No," I said and let out a huge sigh. "Actually, I'm celibate. You coming back to my apartment sounds like an invitation for sex. I decline."

He looked shocked. I imagine he wasn't used to such frankness or not getting what he wanted.

"Really," he said. "For how long?"

I laughed. "Until I'm not."

I got the feeling he wanted me to tell him what it would take for me to break my commitment so he could get what he wanted. It wouldn't be the first time I told a man how to have his way with me.

Not this time.

"Ok," he said, and as expected, his interest waned and eventually evaporated.

We made more small talk, but the direction of the conversation changed. He wasn't in pursuit of me anymore. Part of me was glad because I wasn't sure how strong I could be. I did miss having a man in my life.

But a larger part of me was standing and applauding the fact that I was taking charge of my life.

I thanked Earl for dinner and fought the urge to pay for my meal. I wondered if he felt cheated since he obviously didn't get what he wanted.

I decided that next time I was asked out for a date, I'd lead with the fact that I'm celibate and let them decide if they wanted to proceed with the date. Maybe going dutch wasn't a bad idea either. That way, I wouldn't feel obligated in any way.

I worried needlessly about a 'next time.' My dating life became non-existent. Between working so much and having standards, I wasn't a good catch anymore.

Maybe the only reason I ever was is that I didn't have standards.

That revelation hurt.

A guy I once knew said that men could spot a woman with low self-esteem a mile away.

I was glad to have that target off my back!

Chapter Five: Me Too

'What Now?'

When the 'Me Too' movement came about, I had mixed feelings.

I'd been sexually molested by my obstetrician when I was sixteen. I didn't tell anyone then because I didn't know what had happened.

Who would believe a kid over a professional?

As time went by, that secret became a shame that took root inside of me and made it nearly impossible to speak about.

As I sat and watched the news coverage of the women and girls who came forward telling their truths, I paid attention to the pulse of the people.

Of course, there were those who thought the women were brave for acknowledging their pain publicly. I thought them brave too.

I said nothing, just as I hadn't said anything when it happened.

I put it out of my head then, but I couldn't put it out of my head now.

What had my silence cost another girl?

I had a feeling that I wasn't the first or the last woman he assaulted.

By the time Dr. Onuke molested me, I didn't have any self-value or worth.

Did he know that about me?

How do people like that know that the people they molest have already been silenced?

What made Dr. Onuke do something like that?

Maybe someone had abused him. Maybe it is true that hurt people hurt people.

An old classmate contacted me about publishing her book.

"Iris, I have been trying to get the courage to talk to you for a while now," she said. "I've followed your company on social media. I don't see any books you've done like my story."

"What is your story?" I asked, sensing her uneasiness.

"My story is one of incest and molestation," she said strongly. "I've been having seizures, and the doctors can't figure out why. I've had all the tests, but everything is normal. Finally, my doctor suggested I see a psychiatrist."

Gabby had been very popular in school. I'd envied her because she'd been well developed, and all the boys had flocked around her. The only reason anyone had noticed me was to ask if I knew the answer to a question.

"I'm sorry, Gabby." I offered, and I was. I knew it was frustrating not having answers.

"Thank you, Iris," Gabby said. "You've always been kind. Even as a kid, you were sweet, and I liked you. Do you remember spending the night with my grandmother and me?"

I did remember. It was one of the few times when Mama had left me behind that I hadn't been completely miserable.

"Yes," I said into the phone. "I do remember that."

"I was living with my grandmother because the authorities had gotten involved. A family member had been sleeping with me. I never knew there was a problem. All I knew was that they sent me to live with Grandma. After I left Grandma, I went to live with another family member, and more of the same happened. I graduated high school and found myself doing to a family member what had been done to me. I thought it was normal. By the time I figured out it was wrong, I was ashamed. I tried to forget it and put it out of my head, but according to my psychiatrist, because I haven't worked it all out, my body is adversely affected. Long story short, the doctor feels I'm having these seizures because I haven't dealt with the childhood trauma of being raped by my family member."

Gabby went on to tell me that she was married and had grown children. She said the seizures had gotten so bad she couldn't work or drive. At one point, she and her husband were homeless and had to send their children to a family member to live because they were about to be taken by the state.

My heart went out to Gabby.

I found myself thinking about her children.

Where were they? Who was watching out for them? Were they being cared for?

All the times Mama sent me away, I never rested. By the time she came home, I was exhausted and overjoyed to be in my own bed.

Some of the places Mama left me weren't traumatic, but I was never certain until I left if I'd be safe or not.

I wondered if Gabby thought about that.

Then, I thought about how Gabby was trying to get well, so she couldn't think about the wellbeing of her children.

Was it the same way for Mama?

I'm still not sure where all she was going or what she was doing when she left me places. Maybe she was off trying to feel better.

Now that I'm a mom and grandmother, I understand the need for self-preservation. I know what happens if you don't get it too.

Bad things happen when parents aren't looking.

Whose fault is it? The parent? The perpetrator?

Iris M. Williams

The kid who doesn't tell.

Maybe all of us.

Chapter Six: Connected

'Love Never Leaves'

Besides Mr. Jack, I'd never experienced death up close and personal. The people who had died in my life were not people with whom I'd spent time or had conversations.

When I learned that my brother, Alphonso, had been diagnosed with prostate cancer, I was numb.

Alphonso and I had a past that was fractured at best.

From what I understood, he had been the baby of the family for seven years; then, I was born.

He teased and taunted me and was always making me cry. The things he said were so hurtful. The things he did were just as painful.

"Point at her and call her ugly." Alphonso held our niece, Tracy, on his lap and pulled her close to him. Tracy did what he said, then they laughed.

There was no use in crying or going to tell Mama. I'd learned quickly that telling only made things worse. So, I sat there and pretended it didn't hurt me.

When I found out I was pregnant with my first child, Alphonso had been Mama's partner in crime. Between the two of them, I felt worthless. Mama gave me the silent treatment, while Alphonso unleashed a campaign of insults.

I gained a lot of weight while I was pregnant.

"Tell your brother how much you weigh now," Mama insisted one afternoon after we'd returned from a doctor's appointment.

I felt like I was standing in front of a firing squad. I wanted to be anywhere, but there.

"185," I mumbled.

"A hundred and eighty-five!" Alphonso repeated slowly, enunciating every syllable. "A hundred and eighty-five!" Then, he laughed.

As much as I wanted to hate Alphonso, he was my only connection to Mr. Jack. He and I were Mama's babies by the man she loved so dearly. So, hearing that he had prostate cancer forced me to think about things I didn't want to think about.

Will he die? And what then?

"They say I got this thing, Lil Iris," that Alphonso's pet name for me, "but I know God has me."

At the time, I didn't know God like that, so what he was saying didn't make any sense to me. I kept quiet and let him talk.

"When I get better, I'm going to move down south. I'm going to get me a little house and get a job and bring my children to live with me."

By this time, Alphonso had been through several surgeries and chemotherapy. The cancer had spread to his bones, and he was in a lot of pain. He talked to me frequently, and I could tell he was on pain meds.

"I'm proud of you, Lil Iris," Alphonso told me. "You've always been the smart one."

I was surprised at the things he said to me. I never thought he gave me much thought past contempt.

How come people don't say what they feel when they feel it?

Alphonso never apologized for the things he said and did. Perhaps he never know how

I was affected. I never told him.

But he didn't need to apologize. I figured out that he had seen something in me long before I'd seen it, and at that time, it had threatened him. His wife told me that he spoke highly of me. I never knew or dreamed he would.

Alphonso found Jesus and stood in his rightful place as heir to a kingdom. He knew his worth, and so mine didn't threaten him anymore.

Alphonso fought hard, but in the end, cancer got the last word here on earth. In November of 2013, Alphonso went home to Jesus. In Heaven, I knew Alphonso was taking full advantage of being with God and Mr. Jack!

Days after his funeral, my phone rang, and it was from my dear brother's phone. The phone had already been disconnected. As I sat there and watched his name flash across my screen, I felt like that was his way of letting me know that he hadn't really left.

Love never leaves.

Chapter Seven: Reflections

'The Writing on The Wall'

I've written in a journal or a diary for as long as I can remember. There was something about getting things out of my head and onto paper that was soothing for me.

In preparation for writing this book, I read some of the entries to refresh my memory on what was going on in my life at certain times.

Some things I remembered; others I had forgotten.

The thing about my journal entries that stunned me most wasn't what I wrote, but when I wrote them.

The walls in my life weren't always white and empty. Sometimes there were words, red flags, and warnings. But I never heeded them. I wanted to be in love and to married so badly that I justified what was right in front of me.

The overwhelming theme throughout the years was that I was lonely and tired.

Ironically, it wasn't until I was alone that I found the love I'd been searching for.

October 7, 1988

Sometimes he acts as if he doesn't give a damn. When you love somebody truly, should you consider how your actions will affect them? Sometimes I feel he doesn't love me as much as he says. It's puzzling.

Iris M. Williams

March 6, 1989

Why can't Bradford be as enthused about me as he is about the new car or furniture we have? Maybe it's because of my limp or my weight. I'm so frustrated with myself.

April 28, 1989 – Married Bradford James

(Indiana)

May 1991 – Moved to Arizona

June 29, 1993

My Essence Magazine horoscope says that if I'm doing all the giving, then I should let my mate go. Coincidence or what?

May, 1994 - Moved to Arkansas

July 28, 1994

I'm exhausted. William and I argued again last night. He hurt me by insinuating that I was messing around because I douched. Before him, I'd bathe or shower twice a day, but now I have to stop because he is so irrational and mistrusting.

March 28, 1995 – Divorce #1 Final

May 25, 1995 – Married William White

(Arkansas)

Today, William and I were married. We spent the entire day with his mom. I love William with all my heart, and he is a good man. Right now, I'm lonely. My feelings are hurt. I never dreamed we'd start our lives together this way.

January 18, 1998

I'm tired. I often wonder if the problem lies within me. Can I solve my own problems? Loneliness is such a permanent problem, and the answer is always temporary. I feel like I get slapped in the face daily. It hurts.

The questions are many. My mind wanders. I think too much. I feel too much. It hurts too much. No one understands.

June 21, 1998

I feel so alone, so unloved, so lost, and so confused. I went to church today. I've decided to try God. That means letting go of the fear of being alone. For too long, I've allowed men to use me for sex in exchange for a moment of intimacy for a while.

November 9, 1998

Donald is outside talking to 'his friend.' They've been talking for nearly two hours. I can't get him to talk to me for two minutes because he's too tired or has nothing to say. I'm tired too. I'm tired of loving people who won't even try to love me back. Maybe I'm too picky. I'm old, fat, and crippled, so my options aren't going to be any better than this. How do I swallow my pride, hold my tongue, and look the other way?

November 16, 1999 – Divorce #2

June 30, 2001 – Married Donald Ingram

(Arkansas)

December 31, 2002

It's after 9pm on New Year's Eve, and I'm in my room by myself. My husband is in the living room, entertaining three other men. They are smoking, drinking, and laughing.

What is the point of being married if you have to be alone, go places alone, or spend holidays alone?

October 27, 2003

My days and nights are so lonely. Weekends are the worse. Keeping my feelings to myself does keep the peace on the outside, but it eats me up on the inside. There is no one to talk to about how I feel. I wish I had a close friend.

I am so tired of giving and giving and scraping and begging for love. I push and push and try hard to make things right, but they never end up that way at all. I feel like if I let go, things will fall apart. Just once, I wish someone would hold me together. Just once.

I'm sick of my husband being mean to me. Why does he feel he has the right to talk about me the way he does? Especially since he doesn't talk to me. I'm seriously considering letting go. Holding on is just too hard.

I'm so tired. I'm mad and frustrated. I'm lonely. I've got to be the crazy one to go through this for only a few crumbs of affection. Crumbs are all I get, and maybe crumbs are all I'm worthy of having.

January 5, 2004

Why do I attract the same type of men in my life? Men who are too busy, inattentive, and unresponsive to my needs. I need attention. My friends have several men to meet all their needs. I was stupid to marry one man. I was stupid to marry three times. If this doesn't work, I don't think I'll be able to do it again. I've messed up too much.

Sometimes, you can't recapture lost opportunities.

January 2, 2007

I see the light ahead but wonder if I will ever get to bask in it. So much is going on. So much has happened. And I know there is so much more to come. Some days the thought of what is to come comforts me and excites me. Other days the thought exhausts me because what if it is more of the same?

I'm so lonely.

There does not seem to be anyone who understands or even cares to understand.

I have so much inside of me that longs to come out. Some good. Some bad. Some ugly. Some love, and even some hate.

For more than 30 years, I've held it all in on a promise that I should never have been asked to make.

March 25, 2013 – Divorce #3

(Arkansas)

May 2013 – Moved to North Carolina

November 13, 2013

RIP, my sweet brother Lorenzo (11/10/13). Thank you, Lord, for Lorenzo's spirit, for who he was in my life, and for what he meant. I know you have him now, and he's no longer in pain. My brother is free now and with you and our father, Mr. Jack.

November 12, 2014

I'm such a naive person. I try so hard and give so much only to be disappointed continually. I made dinner and timed it so it would be hot and ready when he got home. It's after 8pm, and he hasn't come home or called. This man is inconsiderate and rude. But I won't say anything because that would just be me being offensive and irritating towards him.

I hate that I have feelings. I wish I could be a cold fish. I'm so tired. I'm so alone.

November 2014 – Moved to Arkansas

November 25, 2014

I'm back in Arkansas. For the first time in my life, I'm truly single. There is a part of me that wishes things were different, but a larger part of me feels this is what is best for me. I've got to learn to stand on my own. I've got to find out who I am. I need to find my purpose.

March 17, 2015

Last night, an angel stopped by. For weeks, I've asked God to send help, and He did. I woke up in the early morning, and instead of turning on the TV, I laid there, still. I waited. Suddenly, I heard 'flapping,' and I saw something 'fly down.' But I don't know what it was. I continued to lay there, thinking that whatever it was would 'fly' back up, but it didn't. I peeked over the side of my bed but saw nothing.

Prophetess said it was an angel, and since I heard the flapping, it was a big one. She said God wanted me to know He is with me and that I'm not alone. She said I have peace in my home, and God knows He is welcomed.

Prophetess told me that I would remarry in 2020. She said everyone would love him, he would adore me, and he would support my dream/life/ministry!

"You're going to happy and joyous," she continued. "It's going to feel as though he came out of the blue. You'll ask him, "Where have you been?"

We laughed.

"Use this time to get prepared for me," She said, knowing that I needed time to heal before I could have a productive relationship with anyone.

January 22, 2017

Lord, free me and make me whole by filling me up with You. And when I'm ready, send me the man You have for me. Open my eyes to him, and in the meantime, keep me safe, secure, and satisfied in You. Lord, I know that You are the source for all my needs, and I don't need anyone but You because You will provide in 'abundance.'

April 11, 2017

I've been celibate for a while now, something I've not been since the age of 15. Wow! I feel special, empowered, and strangely, even loved. I have joy, peace, and even a sense of security. I desire companionship, but I realize I don't 'need' it. I get lonely, but I know I'm never alone. I desire romantic love, but I'm wallowing in agape love. Self-love is everything.

April 13, 2017

Thank you, Jesus, for temptation. It's a gauge and lets me know I need to go deeper in You. Lord, that feeling in the pit of my stomach is smaller, but still there. Will it leave?

Lord, You are my man, so I ask that You protect and keep me.

If only I'd read what I wrote and based decisions on what I knew and not what I felt…

Chapter Eight: Confessions

'Testify'

While I was in North Carolina, Prophetess helped me to reconcile religion and spirituality. In her, I saw the kind of Christian I wanted to be – authentic. I didn't want to hide behind my flaws, but freely acknowledge them so God could heal me.

I appreciated her sense of humor. She was a happy Christian and that made sense to me. She helped me see that loving God makes you happy.

Prophetess was wise too. One thing she said to me was that I had to learn to 'spit out the bones and chew the meat.'

I had no idea what she was talking about.

"You've got to learn to discern what is for you and what isn't," she said and laughed at me as I stood there dumbfounded.

"All good advice is not Godly advice," she said, "and it doesn't all apply to you."

What she said made sense in theory, but it wouldn't be long before I'd understand in practice.

When I arrived from North Carolina, I had a hunger to know God. My daughter was going to a church called *God With Us Who Can Be Against Us Tabernacle of Faith*. She said it was good, so I decided to attend with her.

The church was different than what I'd been used to.

Offering

After each offering, they had you touch the prosperity pole (kind of like on Showtime at the Apollo) on your way back to your seat.

Testimony

And every Sunday before the message, we could stand and give our testimonies on how good God had been to us that previous week.

I wasn't opposed to either of these practices, but there were some things that made me VERY uncomfortable.

Laying Hands

There were times when Pastor Felicia or Pastor Jason would lay hands on someone and pray for them. I'd seen that before. But there were other times when they pulled out the blessed oil. I'd seen that too, but this practice went deeper than anything I'd seen before.

Nina looked weak, sick, tired, and worn out. Her eyes had black circles around them, and she wore an odor that was disturbing to my nose. She wasn't 'musty,' but the odor was unpleasant.

Anyway, she was always being called out by the pastors. They'd lay hands on her and speak in tongues until Nina would cough and throw up! Then, she'd pass out.

Evangelist Smith, Nina's mother, would cover Nina up with a sheet, and service would continue as if Nina wasn't laying prone on the floor. It was very distracting. Finally, she'd open her eyes and get up.

I was very uncomfortable, but I endured it.

However, I decided that if they tried to get me to do that, I'd stop coming to the church!

Pastor Felicia had something else in mind for me.

Praise and Worship

Pastor Felicia was loud and animated, while her husband, Pastor Jason, was more subdued. Typically, Pastor Felicia brought the message, and Pastor Jason prophesied.

Before bringing the Word, Pastor Felicia liked to sing and play the piano.

"Stand to your feet!" She commanded. "Now, give God the praise!"

We'd all stand and begin to sing along with the music.

"Now, raise your hands!" Pastor Felicia demanded.

On this particular day, I didn't feel like raising my hands. I loved God and was glad to be there, but I just didn't feel like raising my hands, so I didn't.

I was in a season of being authentic. I wasn't opposed to raising my hands to show surrender to God. I just didn't feel it.

"Raise your hands!" Pastor Felicia repeated. She seemed to be looking directly at me. The attention was making me uncomfortable, so I raised my hands, and she moved on with the service.

At that moment, I felt like I was a liar. I hadn't raised my hands authentically. I'd only done it because Pastor Felicia had told me to do so. I didn't like how that left me feeling and vowed not to do that again.

The church was small, and Pastor Felicia knew everyone by name. She and Pastor Jason spoke into each of our lives and told us what they saw.

"You're a scribe," Pastor Felicia said. "You've got to learn to be obedient with what God has given you."

I didn't know what a scribe was. So, I said nothing and continued to listen. Then, her husband put his hands on my head, and they prayed. Generally, when this happened, people fell backward. I didn't *want* to fall, but I surrendered myself to the will of God. The longer I stood there, the more pressure he put on my forehead, causing me to become unbalanced.

I fell backward, and Evangelist Smith was behind me to 'help me fall' so I didn't hurt myself. I was taken completely by surprise. I laid there with my eyes closed like I'd seen all the other people do. However, I didn't feel anything but embarrassed and fake.

I didn't like it, and it reminded me of all the times Mama made me 'fix my face,' smile when I didn't want to and go someplace, I hadn't wanted to go. It didn't *feel* real.

I didn't want to participate in anything that wasn't genuine for me.

"Lord," I prayed. "I'll go and do according to Your will. So, if it's Your will, then You cause it to happen. I surrender to You."

Things were fine until one Sunday; Pastor Felicia was running rampant *again* about us raising our hands. It was one of those Sundays where I wasn't in a worshipping mood for whatever reason. I stood and closed my eyes and began silently talking to God. I could hear Pastor Felicia yelling, but I kept my eyes closed and continued to speak to God.

"RAISE YOUR HANDS. GIVE GOD THE GLLLOOOORRRRAAAAAYYYYYY!"

My eyes flew open, and there was Pastor Felicia standing in front of me, yelling.

Embarrassed, I raised my hands. She smirked and walked back to the pulpit.

Had God forsaken me? Why didn't I feel led to raise my hands? Why had Pastor Felicia singled me out?

Later that evening, Pastor Felicia called me.

"Sister Iris," she began, "I'm very disappointed in you. You're letting the devil use you."

"I don't agree, Pastor Felicia," I asserted. It was time for me to stand my ground and to stop letting people tell me what I needed to do, feel, or say. "I was just trying to be real about my worship."

"It ain't about you," she said. "It's about God."

"I didn't feel like praising God that way," I said calmly. "And I'm not gonna do anything I'm not led to do, or that feels fake."

"Well, you must not care about your salvation or the salvation of your family."

"What does my family have to do with this?" I asked, now confused.

"Where you go, so shall your family." She declared.

I took offense to what she was saying. I absolutely wanted my family to get their salvation! Pastor Felicia knew all the words, so I stopped talking.

Had she been right? Was I selfish?

Later, when I spoke with Prophetess about the encounter, she reminded me about the bones.

"I think you're right to want to be God-led in your praise and worship," Prophetess began, "but she was right in that you do have the ability to lead your family. And I can see that you have a scribe's heart. I noticed that when you were here. So much of what you write seems to be from the heart of God. You've told me how there are times when you don't know *how* you know things or *where* the words come from. I believe that's God pouring into your gift. Don't allow Pastor Felicia's tone or misguided antics to prevent you from getting what's yours."

I had told Prophetess that I'd planned to stop going to the church. She told me to pray about it.

I kept going, but as providence would have it, Pastor Felicia and Pastor Jason relocated to another state.

For months, I stayed home, not attending church. My faith in the church had once again been shattered.

Mama's words, never far from my mind, rang clear, "You gotta know the Lord for yourself."

I'd been watching church on TV, but it felt like just a way to check church off a list of things to do. My niece invited me to Rock Creek, and I accepted. I walked in and knew

Iris M. Williams

this was where I was supposed to be.

Chapter Nine: Forgiveness

'I Love You, Mama'

The Church at Rock Creek was good for me. For the first time in my life, I felt good about church, worship, and service. I attended meetings, participated in church activities, and associated with other people who wanted to be intentional and effective about serving God.

I don't believe in coincidences. I believe Rock Creek helped prepare me for what was ahead of me.

"I think Mama is holding on so she can say goodbye to you," my sister, Lola, said.

It wasn't what I was expecting her to say.

Was Mama dying? Did she really care enough about me that she'd put off dying just to say farewell to me?

I wanted to believe it more than I actually believed it.

On the way to her bedside, my emotions were all over the place. Everything kept coming back to the fact that I never got to have what I'd wanted all along — the love of my Mama.

One of the meetings I attended at Rock Creek opened my eyes to the fact that people can only give you what they have.

Was it possible that Mama gave me what she had? Did she love me the way she knew how?

I realized that my current feelings were based on past experiences and a child's understanding (or lack thereof).

Although Mama's words hurt, in some form, they were true. I had been ignorant. I had not understood that love is not always about hugs, kisses, and verbal expressions.

Sometimes, love comes in the form of duty and obligation. My mother took her role as a parent seriously. I was always clean and fed, and she shared her wisdom with me. Yes, I was ignorant to what it all meant, but how many children can understand the wisdom of an adult?

As I walked into the bedroom where Mama laid, years of emotion came up from my belly and stopped at my throat. I still couldn't cry in front of Mama.

Had I been trying to be Mr. Jack's 'big girl,' or had I been trying to mimic my Mama's strength?

Suddenly, none of that was important anymore.

Mama laid in a bed that seemed to swallow her. She was weak and frail, and it pained me to see her in this state. Mama had always been strong. She woke up early and finished more by 7am than most people would do all day.

I never saw her cry.

I certainly never saw her lying in bed well after 3pm. But here she was in bed in her nightgown, and she wasn't on the phone talking to her many friends (something she'd been known for doing).

"Hey, Mama," I was finally able to say. "How are you?"

"I'm ok," she said weakly. "Y'all made it, hunh?"

"Yes, ma'am," I responded. I walked over and leaned down to give her a hug. The mounds of bed cover and fluffy robe didn't hide how much weight she'd lost. My heart continued to break.

Had I missed my opportunity for healing and reconciliation?

The room was silent. I sat and thought about all the times I'd wanted it just to be Mama and me. I'd wanted her undivided attention. Now the time was here, and I felt like my mouth was full of cotton. I had no words or the courage to say them even if they'd been there.

I willed my spirit to get up, to go over to Mama, to hug her, and to tell her that I loved her. But now there were chains on my feet. I continued to sit.

My children talked to Mama freely as I sat there paralyzed. I smiled when it was appropriate - just as I'd been taught.

Finally, my children left the room, but I continued to sit there with Mama. I didn't want to leave her side.

"Come here and hand me the safe," Mama said and motioned under her bed.

"Why?" I questioned and braced myself for a harsh response. But it never came.

"I'm gonna give y'all some money for coming to see me," she said instead.

"No, ma'am," I said, suddenly feeling a shift in the room. Did she think she had to pay me to come see her? "We are ok. We don't need any money."

I was grateful that she was thinking of me. Mama had always been responsible and never wanted to be a burden to anyone. I'd inherited that from her as well.

"I gave Paul some money for you," she said, looking at me, and I felt she could see the pieces of my broken heart. Paul was one of my brothers who was known for being responsible. "The rest of them will be ok, but you - you're my baby."

And that's when my eyes betrayed me. The tears escaped and ran quickly down my face.

I nodded my head vigorously back and forth.

"Yes, ma'am," I said hoarsely, remembering Mama didn't like for you to nod your head. I wasn't ready to have this conversation.

Although Mama didn't apologize or say much more than that, there was a part of me that knew *this* was Mama's way of saying she loved me.

The things my Mama said and did were harsh. Her words had left lasting scars.

I wake up every day, having to remind myself that I am good enough, that I am worthy, and that I am lovable.

I believe in God, which means I believe in the Bible. Believing in the Bible means I believe in what it says. God said there was a plan for my life, which means being born to Mama wasn't an accident.

Maybe God knew that I needed a strong mama in order to survive all the things that were going to happen to me or that I'd get myself into because the truth is, the things Mama did pale in comparison to the things I did to myself.

The choices I made were bad ones. Instead of coming to Christ in a straight and orderly fashion, I took the crooked and winding road. If I'm honest, that road was where I thought I wanted to be because there was something I wanted to have.

I had walked a self-serving journey.

Could it be that the person I needed to forgive was me?

Yes, bad things happened to me that were beyond my control. But what about when I did have control?

Who's to blame for that time?

I'd dreaded this visit with Mama because I wasn't sure what would happen. But as I sat in the room with her, it was as if our spirits were having a conversation. I felt as if a weight was lifted from my shoulders. I no longer needed an apology from her.

I realized I needed to forgive myself.

Later, as I stood to leave, the look in her eyes was sad.

"It looks like its gonna rain," Mama said. "But we need the rain. It hasn't rained in a good while. John (another brother) said he was going to come over here and bring me some fish. The last time he did, I couldn't eat it, but this time I think I can. Lola was supposed to fry me some, but she got them kids to take care of, so I don't want to make more work for her. You should see them kids; they have gotten so big."

Mama was talking fast and rambling. I felt that she didn't want me to leave, and suddenly, I didn't want to leave.

I wished I could go back to being the skinny little girl sitting next to Mama in church. Instead of pushing me away from her, I wanted her to pull me into her softness and allow me to feel love. I wanted to give her love.

I let Mama talk as long as she wanted to.

When she was done, I went over to Mama and allowed her to pull me into her as much as her frail body would allow.

I hugged her back. I put my lips to her ear and whispered the same words to her that I'd said to my baby boy before letting him go.

"I'm sorry."

And I meant it.

Chapter Ten: Giving Love

'Innocence'

Mama made a miraculous recovery! She got up out of that bed, started eating, and was back to living life. I was thrilled. I knew I wasn't prepared for her to leave me. Even though I didn't see her or talk to her, knowing she was here was comforting.

I met Faith in 2016. She found out I was a publisher and told me her daughter was writing a book. We published the book and continued a friendship.

Faith's life was intriguing to me. She seemed to have it all: she was petite, smart, strong, married, and seemed to be doing well in life. She also had what appeared to be a close-knit family.

Being around them highlighted what was missing in my life.

I loved her family and enjoyed being around them. They seemed to take to me too.

"Family," Roger stood and announced one afternoon at dinner. "I have an announcement to make."

I began to feel anxious.

Did I need to excuse myself?

I wasn't part of the family and didn't want to intrude on their privacy.

"From now on, Iris is a part of this family."

My insides felt like they were on the outside. Thankfully, Mama had taught me to 'act,' so I 'acted' cool. But I wanted to scream out in fear.

Why did he do that? What will they think when they know the truth about me?

I didn't know how to accept love. I didn't know if I could trust it. I'd been pulled in only to be tossed aside so many times. I was afraid. Part of me felt I wasn't good enough. These people were beautiful people. They had nice things. I had nothing. I was nothing.

If your Mama couldn't love you, who would?

In my mind, keeping people at a safe distance was the smart thing to do. Too many times, I'd let my guard down only to have my heart ripped out.

I managed to hold back the tears, smile, and mumble, "Thank you so much."

When I finally got in the car, I cried like a baby. I felt joy. I felt sorrow too.

Why couldn't Mama love me like that?

Slowly, I allowed space to distance me from them. I felt it would hurt less if I did it before they did.

I had shared my story with Faith. She had said positive things about it, but I couldn't receive it. I felt she was just kind.

Then, one day out of the blue, she brought my book up again.

She told me about someone she'd met who she thought would benefit from reading my book.

My book? What could my book do for anyone?

"Your story is inspiring. People need to know and see that you can move past the things that happen to you. So, what are you waiting for to publish it?" Faith asked. "I think you should."

I'd learned early on to keep my dreams small to avoid disappointment.

Should I dare dream that big?

"Look," Faith said matter-of-factly. "Tell me specifically WHY you haven't released this book. Because whatever the reasons are, I'll take care of them. I'll help you."

And just like that, she'd removed all barriers, and the only thing I could say was, "Ok."

Weeks later, Faith said, "I've rented a room at the library for your book discussion. We have the room for the entire day. We will have two sessions and a break in between. What do you need me to do?"

I was blown away. Now that someone was managing me and expecting me to produce, I came alive. My interest in my story was renewed, and I felt an overwhelming sense of timing.

The time had come.

I'd told the Lord that I'd do whatever He wanted me to do. It seemed this was what He'd wanted.

In the past, I'd been guilty of 'making things happen' on my own. I was determined this time to wait for God.

I ordered proofs and gave one to Faith, Arie, and Sky. The three of them quickly became my sister-friends. I trusted them. I admired them. We were all different but seemed to share a common bond. I can't say I knew what it was before my book; I just knew it was there.

We met for dinner, and I waited for their feedback.

Would my story be interesting? Would they 'get it'? Could my story make a difference?

It turns out, the common bond we shared was a childhood trauma of some sort. Faith and Arie had positive comments.

"I've told you already that I think you need to publish this," Faith said, rolling her eyes. "You could really make a difference in someone's life. People need to know they are not alone."

I took her comments to heart. Faith was a no-nonsense type of person. She didn't say things she didn't mean.

"When I read your story, it reminded me of a poem I'd written a few years back," Arie said reflectively. "We have to learn to take charge of our lives and to love ourselves first." Then, she performed for us:

> There was a time when the thought of you with her,
>
> my black brother with some other...
>
> made me angry, drove me to anger, made me mad!
>
> Until one day I realized that it just made me sad,
>
> sad for you, sad for me, sad for this society,
>
> who taught you that she was superior and you inferior,
>
> and that somehow being with her made you more,
>
> or, in some strange way, evened the score.
>
> After that epiphany, I knew I couldn't be mad,
>
> because I had work to do.
>
> Not just for you or for me, but for we,
>
> for little black girls who sit behind golden curls
>
> and dream of having The Bluest Eye.
>
> Then go home to Mamas who fry and dye
>
> and braid and weave so that "good hair"

can be achieved.

I've got work to do, until

your being with her no longer

makes you feel superior

and me that much more inferior.

I've got work to do, not just for you or for me…

but for we.

We snapped our fingers. Arie's poetry was deep and so relevant.

"I'll come back to you, Arie," Faith rolled her eyes again. "Because I want to know what's keep you from writing and performing your poetry."

I smiled at Arie. I knew she didn't stand a chance at having a good enough excuse. We both knew that Faith was just looking out for us. She wanted us all to live up to our potential and purpose.

I looked over at Sky. She was quiet, and when she spoke, I got the answers to the questions I'd asked.

"I couldn't put the book down," she exclaimed. "It really held my attention, and I saw so much of myself in your story."

Sky was married and had children. She was also young enough to be my daughter. So, I was wondered if she'd been able to receive my message.

Sky went on to say that she'd had a difficult childhood. Both of her parents were neglectful and withheld love from her.

"My mother was so busy trying to get love from men," she admitted candidly, "she forgot to give her children love. And my father wasn't around to give me love either."

My heart wept for her because I hadn't felt my mother's love either. I admired her honesty. Here she was barely 30 and able to admit what had taken me more than 40 years to admit.

As I have discovered, childhood trauma is not uncommon. Scenes like the one Sky described happens more than I'd care to think. People grow up in homes with one or more parents missing, and not getting what they need for any reason seems to be more normal than not. And no matter the reason (death, divorce, deployment, desertion), it all seems to turn out the same. Absence of love and affection leaves a hole we can spend a lifetime trying to fill.

Sky broke down as she relived the memories. Her wounds seemed as fresh as her tears.

"Now that I'm married and have children, I can see how my childhood trauma impacts my marriage and my ability to parent," Sky admitted. "There are times my husband has to remind me that I'm his wife, not his child."

That truth was received loud and clear. Then, she dropped another bomb.

"My husband is active in our daughter's life, and often times, I find myself being jealous of them."

Like a ton of bricks, I found myself wondering if Mama had been jealous of how Mr. Jack had treated me.

Had Mama been neglected?

Surely, she had. She was only in third grade when she had to quit school and help her family raise kids and chop cotton. She must have felt like a tool for work rather than a child to love.

I could remember when my children were born. I was scared to death of them. I wanted to give them what I had so desperately needed, but I didn't know-how. It was so frustrating.

Somehow, I had pushed through and held them close even when it felt odd. I tried to talk to them, listen, and be there. I colored with them and watched cartoons, partly to bond with them, but also because I never got to do any of that.

I can't remember when I had been carefree and innocent.

How do you give what you don't have?

Forgiveness came for me when I understood that about Mama.

Epilogue: The Truth

'More Precious Than Rubies'

The questions surrounding my life story are many. I wanted to tell my story from the perspective of the person I was. I wanted readers to experience what I experienced – confusion. For most of my life, I had more questions than answers.

Why was Mama so harsh? Why did Mr. Jack have to die? Why did I feel so alone? Why as I not enough?

Although I don't claim to have all the answers now, I can say that I have more than I did. And I believe that the resolution to my problems are found in Jesus.

Probably the number one question I'm asked is, "How did you make it through?"

And my answer is Jesus.

The more I sought after Him, the more answers I received.

Clarity began when I moved to North Carolina. I had a lot of time on my hands, and for the first time since I was fifteen, I had the opportunity to only think of myself.

I hadn't ever liked what I saw in the mirror, so I didn't spend much time there. But in North Carolina, I at least had the time to search myself. I didn't like what I saw there either.

Perhaps the biggest revelation for me was realizing I'd been a liar for most of my life.

I was a people pleaser, doing what others wanted me to do, even when I didn't want what they wanted me to do. I went places I didn't want to go. And I led those around me to believe I was happy to do so. I was afraid of what would happen if I stopped pleasing others.

Would they have a reason to stay around?

Fear and lies governed my life.

In reviewing old journal entries, I notice how I repeatedly wrote of being tired and lonely, even when I was in a relationship.

Fear was why I was tired. It takes works to keep up a lie. Smiling when you don't want to is exhausting.

Fear was also why I was lonely. I was afraid actually allowing people in because they may discover the truth. So, I had to keep them at a distance.

Truth is, I was a hypocrite. I never gave Mama an opportunity to know how I felt. I was too afraid to tell her.

And yet for years, I blamed her for not speaking to me about the things I felt we needed to speak about.

I had to forgive Mama, but I also had to forgive myself for all the things I did and said and for the things I didn't do or say that I should have.

God hadn't given me that spirit of fear.

So, why was I living in fear? Why was I hiding?

Part of the reason I was so afraid was because I knew what I thought of myself. I didn't want others to know. So, I hid and forced myself to become invisible. It worked and for years, I'd gone undetected and unnoticed until I met myself in a mirror.

A mirror reflects who you are. Mirrors reveal two faces – the one you see and the one looking back at you.

Most people run from mirrors for obvious reasons. We don't *really* want to see ourselves. This is evident in the heavy use of photo filters. Ever wonder why Snap Chat is so popular? Check out the filters.

My mirror pulled back the veil and exposed me.

"If you know you deserve more, why are you settling for less?" The mirror asked and waited for an answer.

The question took the wind from me and exposed the first layer of hurt.

How dare it ask me such a thing! Didn't it know that I sacrificed my worth because of my love for it?

The awkward silence felt like a challenge. I felt myself shrink under the scrutiny.

The mirror didn't say anything, but it didn't need to. The question had said it all. The mirror saw me, the real me.

The truth had always been that I settled for less because I didn't *really* believe I deserved more.

A second layer of embarrassment fell away. I attempted a cover up by saying, "I settle because I love you." My voice sounded like the voice of a child. And no wonder, since I was clearly behaving like one.

I went on with a barrage of supporting facts to the "I love you" claim, but the mirror and I both knew it went deeper than that.

Yes, I loved the mirror – deeply, but that wasn't why I settled for less.

"Why are you settling for less if you feel you deserve more?" The mirror wasn't going to let me off the hook. It demanded an answer.

"I settle because you're more important than me," I admitted to myself.

Surely, the mirror knew that. Isn't that why it asked?

But isn't that what love is? I wondered. Isn't that what love does? Don't you sacrifice yourself for love?

The tears came easily now and were a nuisance to me because they didn't offer a release. They were a sign of weakness and defeat. I'd failed to keep this disgusting secret.

"I feel stupid," I said tearfully. The last thing I wanted was to be found in this weakened state.

"You aren't stupid. And you certainly aren't weak."

That wasn't the mirror's response, but I wanted it to be.

Was it because the mirror felt I was stupid and weak?

Insensitivity threatened to chip away at the very foundation of the house that love built. In an effort to hold myself together, I acquiesced to the man in the mirror.

Once again, I surrendered. Once again, I walked away and left a piece of me behind.

Had I turned my back on my worth?

The tears continued. I was too spent to pray. But thankfully, God's grace is sufficient.

The Holy Spirit took over and reminded me of who I am.

"Far more precious than rubies."

The phrase came out of nowhere. And even though I was alone, I heard it clearly. I quickly dried my eyes and typed in the words on my iPhone. Immediatedly, the Proverbs verse displayed: "She is worth far more than rubies."

The words were like water to my dehydrated, wounded, and withering soul.

Is a Proverbs 31 Woman made or is she invented? Is my worth an inheritance that I don't have to earn or is it a fortune to be made?

As the pit in my stomach emptied what I felt and replenished itself with what I knew, I felt myself growing stronger.

Maybe it's a bit of both.

Maybe it's like being handed a robe that's way too big. It's yours, but you have to grow into it.

When I look back over my life at all the relationships I've had (romantic and otherwise), one thing stands out the most.

It has never been the people who I gave myself to who were the problem.

The problem has always been me giving myself away.

So, it never mattered who was on the receiving end – I would always be empty if I gave myself away.

Where did I learn this behavior?

As I continued to read about the Proverbs 31 woman, I saw Mama. I read the passage over and over again and each time, I saw Mama.

- She worked hard.
- She worked farmland and brought home her harvest.
- She worked well into the night after we'd all gone to bed.
- As a single mother, she provided for her children and kept them all.
- She taught her daughters how to serve others.
- She tended a garden and shared its harvest with others.
- She worked vigorously and was strong.
- She gave to the poor.
- She glowed with the light of the Lord.

- She knew how to keep her family warm in winter.
- She could sew and make clothes and quilts.
- She was strong and dignified.
- She was wise.
- She was never idle.
- She feared the Lord.
- Her children call her blessed.

As I read, more tears came as I realized that I as a direct descendant of a Proverbs 31 Woman! Her strength was in me. God saw fit to place me at the feet of this woman to learn how to glorify Him.

I was the daughter of a King and my mother was his Queen.

A Proverbs 31 Woman is worth far more than rubies.

Was I a Proverbs 31 Woman? If I was, why wasn't I behaving as such?

I cried, poured out my heart in pain, but the mirror didn't offer solace. Instead it said, "This doesn't feel like love. This feels like something else."

Is love real if it can't be felt?

My defenses were down. "So, what do I do?" I asked, praying for a solution.

"I can't tell you what to feel or what to do," the mirror continued calmly. "You have to decide what you feel and what you will do if what I offer is not enough for you."

I continued to cry silent, humiliated tears while the mirror twisted the knife. "I don't know how you normally handle your feelings," the mirror said. "So, I'm not sure what to make of this."

For years, I'd shared with the mirror. Yet, it didn't know how I handled my feelings? I realized the mirror only knew the me I'd allowed it to see.

Did the mirror recognize me as precious? Why would it if I wasn't?

I certainly hadn't portrayed myself as such.

"Why do you settle for less, if you know you deserve more?"

That one question broke the final piece of a barrier that held together a fake persona.

And as the walls came down, I saw me.

There is a picture of me as a girl of about six. I'm not smiling and my eyes are sad. For years, I thought it was because no one saw her. No one cared for her. No one valued her. But I realize that little girl was sad because she didn't see herself. She didn't care for or value herself.

Who we are is not a mystery or a secret.

God provided us with a blueprint for knowing who we are and how we are to conduct our lives.

If we follow the plan, we can have what He says we can have.

In seeing myself, I saw my Father, and I began the final stage of metamorphis. As I accepted my heritage, I began to grow stronger.

My tears dried. The pain stopped and my humiliation evaporated.

The prodigal daughter returns home.

My Father runs to me, His precious daughter who is worth far more than rubies, with open arms offering me an abundant life.

When I began this journey, my definition of An Abundant Life would have been about things and people, external factors.

Finally, I understand that An Abundant Life is about knowing who you are, discovering His purpose for your life and pursuing the life that He planned for you.

An abundant life is about reconciling your inside and your outside to where love resides – in Jesus.

I know my purpose. I know my worth.

Knowing that I'm more precious than rubies encourages me to live up to that standard.

Bonus Chapter: Finding Love

'Wonder Twin Power'

The writer's conference was held in Championsgate, Florida, at the beautiful Marriott Hotel. Prophetess, who was also a stylist, was helping me fix my hair. We'd gone down to the hotel pool, and I hadn't been able to resist.

"Sis, what is that you're reading?" She asked.

I'd bought a Christian Romance book to read on the plane. It was so good I couldn't put it down.

"It's by Francine Rivers," I said. "And based on a Bible story."

"Romance in the Bible?" She looked skeptical but then said. "Well, then again, it makes perfect sense. After all, God is perfect love."

"Francine takes Bible stories and imagines what the relationships were like based on what we know to have happened. This book is about Gomer and Hosea and his undying love," I said. "I would love to see it on the big screen."

"You really do love romance, don't you?" Prophetess said and smiled. "Your love will find you when you least expect it."

I wasn't sure about that anymore. Maybe love had passed me by while I was busy making bad choices.

"When I was a kid, there was a cartoon that came on Saturday mornings called Super

Friends. The storyline was about a group of friends who all had different superpowers, but they all had a common goal - to defeat evil and to save the world. Two of the Super Friends were the 'Wonder Twins.' Apart, they didn't possess power, but together, they were insurmountable," I said with a dreamy look. "Even as a kid, I remember thinking how special the Wonder Twins were because unlike the other superheroes, they had a partner. They had to work together and be one in order to accomplish anything great. I want a love like that. A love that I can depend on, and instead of pulling me down, it will lift me up, and together, we will soar."

That kind of sentimentality has always been a part of who I am.

Before I went to school and learned to read, as an only child, I'd spend hours alone making up conversations with people who weren't there.

Then when I got to school and the teacher would read to us (and then show us the picture), I was completely involved and hated when the reading circle was over because I wanted to know what happened. I'd go home and imagine an ending.

Quickly I discovered that I preferred my ending over the actual ending. Even to this day, when I watch a movie or read a book, I can often predict the ending. I walk away thinking, "I could have done that. But I would have done it like this or that."

After years of being obsessed with words, finding myself as an author and publisher wasn't much of a stretch. It seems I was destined to be one. I love what I do and would do it for free (I practically do) if I could. For me, there is nothing more satisfying than taking words and shaping them into something that moves people to feel, act, or respond.

And for most of my life, I had never met anyone who felt the same.

Until Raymond Melbourne.

After the conference, the Prophetess and I were having dinner in the hotel's restaurant. She noticed Raymond right away.

"Sis, look at that man over there," she nodded her head, and I followed her gaze. "What you think about *that*?"

The man she was pointing to was very handsome. But I'd never had a 'type' of man that I was attracted to based on how he looked. I was more stimulated by a man's mind.

"He's very handsome," I said offhandedly, but I quickly dismissed him. Besides, I never wanted to contend with was an overly handsome man. Who wanted to have to fight off the women who were bold enough to ignore wedding bands? Not me!

"Yes, he is," she continued, "but look what he is doing."

I had shared with the prophetess that I was looking for someone to work with me. I needed more than an editor. I needed someone who was as passionate about words as I was.

I looked again and noticed that he was furiously marking papers. From where we sat, it looked like he was grading or editing them. His glasses were on the tip of his nose, and the pen he held was red.

Interesting.

Then, he looked up. Our eyes met, and he smiled. I smiled back. From across the room, I felt a *knowing* that I had never experienced before. It was charging and left me feeling unsteady.

He removed his glasses, got up and walked over to our table.

"Hello," he said, extending his hand to Prophetess while looking at me. She shook his hand; then, he extended his hand towards me. "Good evening. My name is Raymond Melbourne. How are you ladies this evening?"

As much as I loved words, they escaped me.

"I noticed that you're dining alone," he continued. "Would you mind if I joined you? If you say yes, I'll spring for dessert."

Prophetess loved sweets and immediately said, "Yes, that would be wonderful."

Raymond went back to his table, expertly gathered his items into what looked like a very expensive leather case and made his way to our table.

The waiter came, set an extra setting and took our dessert order. I felt like I was in a trance of some sort. My palms were sweating, and my heart was racing. He was in my space, and it seemed he was taking up all the air in the room. This man was larger than life, but his eyes were kind.

"I have a confession," he said and leaned forward without taking his eyes off me. "I have an agenda."

I knew it. This was already too good to be true.

"What is that you want?" Prophetess asked and smiled a huge smile. She must have already had a 'sense' about this man.

"I'm a writer, and I noticed that you two are as well," he began.

"How do you know that?" I blurted out. Finally, I could speak.

"The badges that you're wearing," he said and pointed as I looked down. I felt foolish. We were still wearing our Writers Conference laynards.

"I'm a writer, but this lady right here is the one you want," Prophetess said with a glint in her eye. "She is actually a publisher and an author."

"Oh really," he said and seemed to move in even closer. "Today must be my lucky day."

"There is no such thing as luck or coincidence," Prophetess said.

And in unison, they both said, "It has already been written."

We all laughed, and the tension subsided for me. Raymond had a beautiful smile. He was clean-shaven and had a receding hairline that only served to create a distinguished look. When he turned his head to speak to Prophetess, I took the opportunity to look him over from head to toe. Impeccably dressed and fit, I was starting to feel myself become intimidated.

As he spoke, I found comfort in his soothing voice. I could listen to him speak all day.

"So, Ms. Williams," he smiled as he read my name. "Or is it Mrs. Williams?"

"It's Ms.," I confirmed. "But you can call me Iris."

"Iris it is," he said and took my hand. "If you'll call me Raymond." Then, he pulled my hand up to his lips and kissed it so gently; I wasn't sure if he did or if it was my imagination.

I nodded my head. My voice seemed to have left me again.

"Speak up! I heard Mama's voice. Don't act like a deaf-mute!"

"Raymond, it is," I said and shook my head, trying to free myself of Mama's harsh voice.

"I'm a Professor of Literature over at Florida State. I'm here having an early dinner and was grading some papers when I noticed you two walk in. Perhaps it is fate, since as you looked my way, I felt a strong and unusual urge to introduce myself. And I see now that I was right. I needed to meet you, Iris."

Prophetess clapped her hands like she was watching a Hallmark movie. Raymond and I looked at her and laughed.

"And why exactly is that?" I asked curiously.

"Because I've written a romance novel and need someone to read it and give me honest feedback. If it's good enough, I'd like to publish it too."

"Isn't that something," Prophetess declared. "Iris loves romance. It's her favorite genre! And didn't you tell me that you were looking for a male romance author?" She said excitedly, squeezing my arm too tightly.

I looked at her and wondered why she seemed so eager about *this* man and *his* work. But she was right. I had mentioned to her that I was looking for someone who could write stories like the Hallmark movies that I loved so much, but from a male perspective.

"There seems to be a lack of romance in the world," I'd complained. "That's why Hallmark is my favorite channel. I want a love like that."

"It'll find you," Prophetess had assured me. "You've just got to be patient and wait for it."

Waiting had never been my strong suit. But after all I'd been through, I knew that it was time I moved out of God's way and let Him send me the man that He made just for me.

"What's your story about?" I asked Raymond. "And what makes it different from any other love story?"

"Well, first, it was given to me by God. I'm just His vessel. The story belongs to Him," he said with such passion and certainty, I already knew I'd love it.

I sat and waited for him to tell me more.

"People have love all wrong these days. They think it's something you receive or fall into, but it's actually something you share. When it comes to romantic love, the best kind is the kind that you share when you become one with a person. When you meet that person that was made for you, together, you become something great. You two ladies may be too young to remember this, but do you remember a Saturday morning cartoon called Super-Friends?"

Prophetess teeth threatened to escape her mouth and her smile grew even wider.

I nodded in recognition, then quickly spoke up to avoid hearing Mama's critical voice in my head about not speaking.

"Yes," I said. "I remember the Justice League."

"Well, I'm looking for the other half of me. I'm looking for the woman who, with me, we possess a force that is impenetrable. I'm a man after God's own heart and I'm searching for a woman whose worth is far more than rubies. I'm looking for my Wonder-Twin."

A wave of emotion came over me, and I felt myself smiling from the inside out.

In unison, he and I said, "Activate." Then, we all laughed again.

The restaurant had a spot for dancing out on the patio. A Bobby Womack song came on, and I heard Raymond gasp.

"That's one of my favorite songs," he exclaimed. "Prophetess, if the lady will permit me, would you excuse us while we take a swirl around the dance floor?"

Prophetess nodded; then, Raymond held out his hand and assisted me as I stood.

Sparks flew, and I felt my smile grow wider. On the dance floor, he pulled me in close to him, and I marveled at how perfectly I fit in his arms.

Love has finally come at last, and I'm never gonna give it back ...

Raymond sang in my ear. His voice was overpowering Bobby Womack's rendition.

He held me tight and I felt his heart beat against mine. Or was my heart beating against his? His breath was warm in my ear as he sang. I laid my head on his chest and felt safe. I felt at home.

I felt myself falling in love.

BUZZ

BUZZ

BUZZ

My alarm clock buzzed, and my eyes flew open. For a minute, I didn't know where I was. As the realization came over me, I smiled.

For years my dreams had been nonexistent. When I closed my eyes at night, there had been nothing but blackness.

Could it be I had regained hope?

I was encouraged by that thought and my acceptance of my past. I was no longer ashamed, fearful, or hopeless. I now embrace my past because it helped shaped who I am today.

Iris M. Williams

I accept the fact that I'll always hear Mama's voice. Her influence will always be with me.

I'll temper her words with Prophetess's advice to "Chew the meat but spit out the bones."

Not everything Mama said was negative. There was wisdom in her words. I simply didn't understand the relevance of it at the time.

On this side of life, I know that Mama loved me. She gave what she had.

I'm ready to live and love, at last.

About the Author

Growing up in a small rural town in Arkansas, Iris M. Williams experienced life in its simplest form. However, her life was anything but simple.

For most of her life, she felt she was in a fog of questions for which there were no answers.

Although she was an avid reader from a young age, she never found herself or her life between the pages of her beloved books. Those happy stories were about other people, people who didn't look like she did.

Although she couldn't identify with the people in the books she read, she could escape the pain and disappointment that was her life.

In the final book of a three-part series, the author invites readers to look forward, to acknowledge the past, to heal, and to view their life based on who they are today. She encourages you to envision the life you want and make it happen!

By sharing her story, Iris hopes that readers can see themselves, and instead of escaping their reality, learn to face it so that healing and growth can occur.

To contact or learn more about the author, visit her website:

www.irismwilliams.com

A Poem: This Woman's Work

There was a time when the thought of you with her,
My black brother with some other...
Made me angry, drove me to anger, made me mad!
Until one day I realized that it just made me sad,
Sad for you, sad for me, sad for this society
Who taught you that she was superior and you inferior,
And that somehow being with her made you more,
Or in some strange way evened the score.

After that epiphany, I knew I couldn't be mad,
Because I had work to do.
Not just for you or for me, but for we.
For little black girls who sit behind golden curls
And dream of having The Bluest Eye.
Then go home to Mamas who fry and dye
And braid and weave so that "good hair"
Can be achieved.

For little black boys who'll grow up to be men
In a world that counts them as statistics,
More likely to spend time in the pen
Than to pick up a pen and write great books,

That you know Black folks won't read anyway,

Or so they say.

And it saddens me deeply that The Mis-Education of the Negro

is just as relevant today!

I've got work to do, not just for you or for me,

But for we. . .

For we the people who continue to perpetuate the myths and the lies,

With blue, green, and hazel contact-lensed eyes,

Because we just don't see the beauty of our own, deep dark brown.

For my people who have fallen victim to ourselves,

And feel so trapped in this present hell

That we try to buy our way out with material possessions,

Our own new obsessions,

From wheels to grills,

Just to prove who we are or announce that we've arrived

But remain too ignorant, to recognize our own strength and power.

I've got work to do, not just for you or for me,

But for we. . .

So that my young daughter

Will grow up remembering the lessons that I taught her.

That nappy is GOOD

And Black is Beautiful

And regardless of your 'hood

You can still represent to the fullest

And it's cool to be smart,

It's alright to follow your heart,

But never forget where your head is.

And by knowing all of this,

She will know self-love and won't

Need to look for it in all the wrong places,

Or compare herself to the many different faces

On television and in magazines

Promoting a beauty standard based on superiority

And embedding a feeling of inferiority

That runs way too deep and keeps

Me standing here today torn between anger and sadness.

I've got work to do, until

Your being with her no longer

Makes you feel superior

And me that much more inferior.

I've got work to do, not just for you or for me. . .

But for we.

Cassie (Miller) Hartaway

A Poem: Relationship Status

If I were in a relationship, I'd treat him like a King.
Then, why don't I live like a Queen?

If I were in a relationship, I'd gladly make him something to eat.
So, why don't I nourish myself,
instead of now and then as a treat?

If I were in a relationship, I'd care for him and love him gently.
So, why don't I care for myself in all ways, completely.

If I were in a relationship, I'd be there for him –
he wouldn't have to ask.
So, why don't I shower myself in love,
better yet why in it don't I bask?

If I were in a relationship, I'd love him as I love myself.
So, doesn't that mean I need to treat me as if I'm kept?

If I were in a relationship, affection upon affection I'd never spare.
So, shouldn't I practice personal self-care?

If I were in a relationship, I'd shower him with material things.
So, why do I deny myself the pleasure finer things can bring?

If I were in a relationship, he'd be a priority.

So, shouldn't my priority list also include me?

If I were in a relationship, I'd need to be whole.

So, why aren't I waiting for the one with whom I share a soul?

If I were in a relationship, he would be my King.

So, why would I ever settle for less than being Queen?

Iris M. Williams

Whatever Happened To …

We gravitate towards who we are inside.

When I was sick, I attracted people who highlighted my sickness. I believe God designed it that way for us to confront and resolve our issues.

However, instead of looking at me, I blamed them. I put the focus on them instead of dissecting me to figure out why I felt and behaved the way I felt and behaved.

Yes, people do and say things to hurt us, but how we respond is more about us than them.

When I read my journal entries, I realized that before each marriage, I'd seen the warning signs and had ignored them all.

I knew what those marriages would bring, and instead of making a choice that was healthy for me, I gave my power away. I never felt like I deserved anything better than what I was being offered.

I didn't know that I was a Proverbs 31 woman and that my worth was far more precious than rubies.

Even though those relationships didn't last, they were successful in that they served as gold bricks on my road to Oz.

In my books, I highlighted the bad parts of my relationships to make a point. As we know, nothing is all bad or all good. I believe the people who hurt me didn't do so on purpose. Maybe they were sick too.

In speaking with readers about books I and II, there were questions asked that I wanted to answer here in the final book.

Benny Pete left our small town and enlisted in the military. Years later, he and I had an opportunity to talk about what happened, but too much time had passed to recapture what may have been. He is married and living on the west coast.

Alisha's dad died in 2014 from cancer. He had been in prison, and the two of them had corresponded through letters. I was happy that she had those letters in the end.

I never spoke to **Jamie's** dad again. I only had his 'nickname,' so I couldn't search for him on Social Media. Anyway, what would I say?

Bradford married again, but is now divorced. He had two other children, and he and our son, BJ, are in touch on a regular basis.

I heard **William White** is now a pastor of a church. Part of me wonders about his sincerity, but I do know that people can change, and God does work miracles.

Donald Ingram is a good man. He has stayed in contact with my children and my grandchildren. There was the hope of a reconciliation, but I didn't see much in the way of change and decided it was better not to repeat bad habits.

Malcolm got divorced and plans to retire from the military. I saw him a few times after moving back to Arkansas, but things never felt the same. Too much had been said and done to ever go back.

Gregg and I don't talk anymore, but I know I can call him, and he'd be a friend. He successfully battled cancer and called me after the fact to report his miracle and to tell me that he's finally going to remarry. I'm happy for him.

After seeing **Anton** in the grocery store, a few months after he left without saying goodbye, he called and begged me to let him come back. By that time, I was talking to William, so I didn't entertain it, but if I'm honest with myself, I probably would have agreed if I'd been alone. Sadly, that's just how low my standards were.

Mr. Jack died just as I became comfortable having him in my life. I was in my twenties when I found out by accident that he didn't live with us. In fact, he was married to someone else, which explained why I was taught to call him Mr. Jack (among other things). Maybe some of my animosity should have been directed towards him, but he was dead, and Mama wasn't. I still haven't grieved him.

Mama has health issues that are challenging to manage and even more difficult to witness. Admittedly I'm not doing a good job with accepting what is or maximizing the time I have. When others counted her out, she reminded them of how strong she is, and I thank God for that. Mama sowed plenty of good seeds when she could and now, she's living off that harvest. Her illness prevents us from having the conversation I'd like us to have, but maybe it isn't necessary anymore. Through forgiving myself and Mama, I can finally appreciate her.

And as for **me**, I turned 50 in July of 2019. It was a quiet and uneventful day. I worked that day, had dinner with my children that evening and was home in bed by 10 pm that night.

I'd always thought that turning 50 would be a momentous event celebrated with lots of food, fun, and friends. It wasn't.

I don't have a husband or a boyfriend.

But I have found love.

It's been more than five years since I returned to Arkansas from North Carolina – broken and absent of hope.

During that time, I've learned to cry, to speak, and I'm seeking an authentic life. I desperately want to live the life I speak about.

I falter and have setbacks, but the recovery time gets shorter and shorter.

The team around me is strong, supportive, and refuses to let me isolate for too long.

I'm grateful.

"The thief comes only to steal and kill and destroy.

I came that they may have life

and have it abundantly."

John 10:10

Eiffel Tower Books is an imprint of Butterfly Typeface Publishing.

Little Rock AR

www.butterflytypeface.com

www.ingramcontent.com/pod-product-compliance
Lightning Source LLC
Chambersburg PA
CBHW060501240426
43661CB00006B/872